P9-DHD-771

Teaching for Justice

Concepts and Models
for Service-Learning
in **Peace Studies**

Kathleen Maas Weigert and Robin J. Crews, volume editors

Edward Zlotkowski, series editor

A PUBLICATION OF THE

AMERICAN ASSOCIATION
FOR HIGHER EDUCATION

Teaching for Justice: Concepts and Models for Service-Learning in Peace Studies
(AAHE's Series on Service-Learning in the Disciplines)
Kathleen Maas Weigert and Robin J. Crews, *volume editors*
Edward Zlotkowski, *series editor*

ISBN 1-56377-015-6
ISBN (18 vol. set) 1-56377-005-9

Contents

Part III:
Service-Learning Courses in Peace Studies

Appendix

About This Series

by Edward Zlotkowski

The following volume, *Teaching for Justice: Concepts and Models for Service-Learning in Peace Studies*, represents the 10th in a series of monographs on service-learning and academic disciplinary areas. Ever since the early 1990s, educators interested in reconnecting higher education not only with neighboring communities but also with the American tradition of education for service have recognized the critical importance of winning faculty support for this work. Faculty, however, tend to define themselves and their responsibilities largely in terms of the academic disciplines/disciplinary areas in which they have been trained. Hence, the logic of the present series.

The idea for this series first surfaced late in 1994 at a meeting convened by Campus Compact to explore the feasibility of developing a national network of service-learning educators. At that meeting, it quickly became clear that some of those assembled saw the primary value of such a network in its ability to provide concrete resources to faculty working in or wishing to explore service-learning. Out of that meeting there developed, under the auspices of Campus Compact, a new national group of educators called the Invisible College, and it was within the Invisible College that the monograph project was first conceived. Indeed, a review of both the editors and contributors responsible for many of the volumes in this series would reveal significant representation by faculty associated with the Invisible College.

If Campus Compact helped supply the initial financial backing and impulse for the Invisible College and for this series, it was the American Association for Higher Education (AAHE) that made completion of the project feasible. Thanks to its reputation for innovative work, AAHE was not only able to obtain the funding needed to support the project up through actual publication, it was also able to assist in attracting many of the teacher-scholars who participated as writers and editors.

Three individuals in particular deserve to be singled out for their contributions. Sandra Enos, former Campus Compact project director for Integrating Service With Academic Study, was shepherd to the Invisible College project. John Wallace, professor of philosophy at the University of Minnesota, was the driving force behind the creation of the Invisible College. Without his vision and faith in the possibility of such an undertaking, assembling the human resources needed for this series would have been very difficult. Third, AAHE's endorsement — and all that followed in its wake — was due largely to then AAHE vice president Lou Albert. Lou's enthusiasm for the monograph project and his determination to see it adequately supported have been critical to its success. It is to Sandra, John, and Lou that the monograph series as a whole must be dedicated.

Another individual to whom the series owes a special note of thanks is Teresa E. Antonucci, who, as program manager for AAHE's Service-Learning Project, has helped facilitate much of the communication that has allowed the project to move forward.

The Rationale Behind the Series

A few words should be said at this point about the makeup of both the general series and the individual volumes. Although peace studies may seem the most natural of all disciplinary areas with which to link service-learning, the volume's editors themselves point out that these two interest areas have only recently discovered each other. Furthermore, "natural fit" has not, in fact, been a determinant factor in deciding which disciplines/interdisciplinary areas the series should include. Far more important have been considerations related to the overall range of disciplines represented. Since experience has shown that there is probably no disciplinary area — from architecture to zoology — where service-learning cannot be fruitfully employed to strengthen students' abilities to become active learners as well as responsible citizens, a primary goal in putting the series together has been to demonstrate this fact. Thus, some rather natural choices for inclusion — disciplines such as anthropology, geography, and religious studies — have been passed over in favor of other, sometimes less obvious selections from the business disciplines and natural sciences as well as several important interdisciplinary areas. Should the present series of volumes prove useful and well received, we can then consider filling in the many gaps we have left this first time around.

If a concern for variety has helped shape the series as a whole, a concern for legitimacy has been central to the design of the individual volumes. To this end, each volume has been both written by and aimed primarily at academics working in a particular disciplinary/interdisciplinary area. Many individual volumes have, in fact, been produced with the encouragement and active support of relevant discipline-specific national societies. In the case of this Peace Studies volume, the Peace Studies Association has been most helpful.

Furthermore, each volume has been designed to include its own appropriate theoretical, pedagogical, and bibliographical material. Especially with regard to theoretical and bibliographical material, this design has resulted in considerable variation both in quantity and in level of discourse. Thus, for example, a volume such as Accounting contains more introductory and less bibliographical material than does Composition — simply because there is less written on and less familiarity with service-learning in accounting. However, no volume is meant to provide an extended introduction to service-learning *as a generic concept*. For material of this nature, the reader is referred to such texts as Kendall's *Combining Service and Learning: A Resource Book for Community and Public Service* (NSIEE, 1990) and Jacoby's *Service-Learning in Higher Education* (Jossey-Bass, 1996).

I would like to conclude with a note of thanks to Kathleen Maas Weigert and Robin J. Crews, coeditors of this volume. Their willingness to respond to suggestions from various quarters has helped make this a text that effectively speaks to the heart of service-learning's commitment to more just, more humane social vision. I would also like to acknowledge the generous assistance of Dale Bryan, of Tufts University, and Steven Trainor, of Rivier College, who provided valuable feedback on the manuscript.

May 1999

Preface

by Elise Boulding

The story of how two separate learning communities with a strong normative orientation to social policy and social betterment have in recent years come to collaborate is a tale that needs to be told. Both peace studies and service-learning have been developing new conceptualizations of how social learning takes place as a community process in situations of conflict and what the dynamics of peace building are. This has created a new niche in academia for preparing students to become social change agents.

In retrospect, it is perhaps not surprising that peace studies and service-learning developed independently. Peace research and undergraduate peace studies programs grew out of the frustrations of social scientists with the intellectual freeze of the Cold War and the accompanying inability of international relations as a field to focus on systems change and broader concepts of peace and security. Service-learning has many antecedents. One is the Outward Bound schools that began in England 50 years ago, training young boys in rescue missions in a community-based approach to education. Outward Bound programs can be found today in academia within schools of education, offering "expeditionary learning." The post-World War I international work camp movement — Service Civile Internationale — might be thought of as another antecedent. Young people in the work camp movement flocked to summer and year-round field service projects in social reconstruction, but usually outside of academia. Training needs for the various national service and Peace Corps types of programs after World War II also played a role in focusing attention on such activities not only as service opportunities but also as settings for learning.

However, it was not until the 1970s that serious recognition of service-learning as an educational enterprise suitable for college campuses took place. Finally it came to be seen that peace studies and service-learning needed each other. It was the concept of experiential community-based learning for social change practitioners that provided the bridge linking the two communities within the academic world. This linkage provided legitimization for what some of us in peace studies had been doing all along — sending our students into adjacent towns and cities to work for local chapters of international nongovernmental organizations, thus learning how global networks operate at the local level.

1990 Nobel Peace Prize nominee Elise Boulding is professor of sociology emerita at Dartmouth College. One of the founders of the International Peace Research Association, she is a pioneer in the fields of women's studies, peace research, and futurism as a scholar, author, and activist.

This stimulating book gives a picture of what is going on right now in this exciting break with formalistic academic studies, as exemplified in the different college and university programs and courses, undergraduate and graduate, here described. Most of the academic settings are secular, but the powerful peace and justice orientation of the historic peace churches and the Catholic peace movement shines through as a strong moral force in the new peace studies and service-learning nexus. The traditional assumption that the teaching of theory must rigidly precede practice in real-life situations is shown to be false. These programs and courses demonstrate that immersion in field situations of conflict and violence can generate theoretical insights and intellectual analysis of conflicts even while cultural empathy with communities at risk is simultaneously developing.

This type of learning recalls the Paulo Freire model of teachers-as-learners and learners-as-teacher and involves a profound respect for the capacity of students to respond to the complex challenges of real-life situations. This approach also places a strong emphasis on the personal development of each individual student, particularly through the continual practice of journalizing and reflection. Interestingly, personal development and capacity for intellectual analysis are seen to go hand in hand. Intellectual rigor is emphasized in each program, but so is personal maturity and hands-on peace-building skills.

The in-depth exposure to unfamiliar life settings in service-learning — particularly situations of violence, poverty, and oppression — invariably has a profound effect on students. They discover very soon that they have a lot to learn from those they are working with and that the only viable relationship is one of partnering, rather than of being an outside do-gooder. This will have profound consequences for their ways of working after completing their studies.

Each program and course described in this book represents a unique patterning and balancing of the needs for theory and practice, for intellectual maturing, for reflection and personal development, and for various kinds of skill building in a variety of settings around the world. It is exciting to see how many forms such programs and courses can take. Every teacher, in reading these accounts, will be stimulated to think about developing a version of peace and social change learning that will fit his or her institutional setting. Every instructor will also find grounds for presenting the intellectual and moral legitimacy of a service-learning approach to peace studies. Problems and difficulties in finding and developing community service sites are frankly discussed, as is the need for enough support staff to stay in touch with agencies in the field, to ensure authentic service-learning experiences. These programs and courses are demanding, not only for students but for faculty as well! But the enthusiasm of these authors gives us all as reader-participants a new vision of what is possible on college campuses in community-based peace and service-learning at a time when the world is crying out for peace-building skills.

Introduction

by Kathleen Maas Weigert and Robin J. Crews

This volume provides essays on the integration of service-learning into the field of peace studies. Although peace studies and service-learning (SL) have unique origins, they also have some similar goals and, if you will, a similar spirit. In this introduction we provide the reader with, first, a general guide to the key issues we think arise with the coming together of the two fields; second, some comments about what peace studies has to offer service-learning; and third, an overview of what the reader will discover in the essays that follow.

Peace Studies and Service-Learning: Key Issues at the Intersection

At least three key issues emerge in the interstitial territory occupied by peace studies and service-learning: social change, the prevention of war and violence, and community impact. The first two are more specific to the peace studies and service-learning territory and are interrelated, while the third is a common concern to service-learning in general. As the reader will note, the thread of social change — the study of fundamental alterations in societal structures, behavior, and beliefs over time — is woven into this volume. From the beginning, practitioners of peace studies pedagogies have been concerned with images of a more just and peaceful world and vitally interested in finding ways to effect such a vision (Boulding 1990; Brock-Utne 1985; Harris 1996; Hicks 1988; Lakey 1987; Lopez 1989; Reardon 1988; Salla et al. 1995). Certainly, cognate fields (sociology and international relations, for example) have had social change as one of their central concerns; various models have been put forth, scrutinized, and debated since their beginnings. The ideas of such giants as Comte, Marx, Weber, and Spencer, among others, have given shape to many of the concerns that still dominate contemporary discourse. Peace studies professionals entered into these discussions as well, with particular emphasis on peace movements and nonviolent struggles as vehicles of social change at the macro level (Ackerman and Kruegler 1993; Carter 1992; Powers and Vogele 1997; Sharp 1973, 1990). The life and works of such exemplars as Leo Tolstoy, Jane Addams, Mohandas K. Gandhi, A.J. Muste, and Martin Luther King, Jr., provide fertile ground for conceptualizing and concretizing models of peaceful change (Bondurant 1965; DeBenedetti 1986).

Obviously, no one model dominates the work on social change in general or on peaceful social change in particular. What the reader will find woven into the following essays are glimmers of various models, as the authors struggle with the relationships between service-learning and peaceful social change. Perhaps what most clearly emerges is the contemporary emphasis on the micro level, with its focus on the role of the individuals who, by getting involved in collaborative projects with others (often through community organizations), offer their ideas and efforts to advance a cause larger than themselves, and who reflect on the implications of such efforts to bring about change (see Weigert 1989). In the field of peace studies, many would typically categorize the substantive areas most of the authors discuss and employ in their teaching as instances of "positive peace" (Galtung 1964), that is, structures and processes that allow for greater justice, more inclusive participation in decision making, and greater equality in the distribution of resources.[1]

Some of the authors, perhaps most specifically Bing and Blechman, focus on efforts toward what Galtung (1964) calls "negative peace," that is, the absence and prevention of war and, by extension, the absence and prevention of violence. We think that the penchant in this volume toward SL placements in agencies with "positive peace" agendas reflects quite accurately the state of the field at this time. Although there are examples of experiential learning (EL) as opposed to SL activities[2] that relate to negative peace (see, for example, Bing 1989; Weigert 1990), more SL efforts are directed toward enhancing justice and human development (than to mitigating direct violence and war) quite simply because such opportunities are more abundant locally, fit with the Zeitgeist, and are appealing to both students and faculty alike. As the use of SL in peace studies grows, we expect to see more service-learning experiences related to international aggression and conflict, arms trade, low-level intensity conflicts, nuclear weapons, and the like — the standard fare at the theoretical and empirical research levels but not yet at the pedagogical level. This will take concerted efforts by practitioners. It will also launch them head-on with the charge of "ideological bias," i.e., the claim that those who get involved in such work are doing "political" or "liberal" work that is camouflaged as academic work — a charge waged more broadly against the use of comparable placements in service-learning as a whole (see Weigert's essay in this volume, as well as Saltmarsh 1998).

The third key issue, as noted above, is more generic to service-learning across the disciplines: the impact of SL efforts on the community (communities). What are the results of service-learning efforts in and on the community? How are the results assessed? We do have anecdotal evidence that agencies find student placements to be important in meeting the needs of the people the agencies serve. We also have the evaluation of Learn and

Serve America (Melchior 1998: 61), which found that agency representatives, in almost every case, "spoke positively of the work of the students and the contributions that they had made." But Melchior (1998: 65) also reports that one-third of the agencies said that "all of the work" completed by student volunteers would have been done without them. This is a topic that calls for much more study (see Giles and Eyler 1998). The expanding field of participatory action research is one area in which these issues are being addressed (Whyte 1991; Nyden et al. 1997).

Peace Studies' Contributions to Service-Learning

Based on our own teaching and on conversations with colleagues in and from both fields, it appears to us that peace studies brings at least three central concerns to service-learning. First and foremost is the focus on justice. As the title of this volume suggests, "justice" is fundamental to peace studies and, as such, perhaps offers a sharper focal point to SL. How so? One of the critiques of SL is that it tends to "fit" people into existing structures and processes, to make such arrangements work better; in short, SL can be a status quo endeavor. Conceptually, peace studies asks the questions: Are the current processes and structures "just"? Who is harmed by the existing system? How might it be altered to allow for greater justice? Questions such as these encourage SL practitioners to be more explicit about their long-term goals.

Coupled with this focus on justice is the importance of nonviolence in bringing about grass-roots social change. Here, the emphasis of conflict resolution programs in schools and neighborhoods is perhaps the most concrete and localized manifestation of the concern for reducing the resort to violence to settle differences. From schools (Lantieri and Patti 1996) to neighborhoods (McGillis 1997; Schwerin 1995), it is clear that more groups and communities are interested in helping their members learn skills needed for working with conflicting interests while minimizing violence. The good news is that there are growing sets of tools and research findings to be explored. As the reader will see, the development of skills is often tied into service-learning placements in peace studies courses.

Third and related, peace studies asks SL to think more explicitly about the larger context in which SL occurs. Peace studies practitioners, while often focusing on a local setting, are committed to raising local-global connections so that students see their embeddedness in a larger network of relationships. The neologism *glocal* captures this perspective.

Overview of Essays

We turn now to an overview of the contributions to this monograph and note that some (but not all) of the essays include "tools" and most (but not all) include bibliographic references that we think will be of use to the reader. The first section focuses on theoretical and conceptual issues that undergird and shape the territory occupied by peace studies and service-learning. Weigert begins with a theoretical examination of a "moral" obligation of peace studies pedagogy to help prepare students to lead engaged, committed lives in a global context; she argues that EL in general and SL in particular offer important vehicles for meeting that central goal. In a more autobiographical essay, Crews examines how peace studies and SL come together and what that combination can contribute to the reform of the academy as well as to social change in society at large. Schratz and Walker conclude this section with an examination of the inner workings of service-learning as social learning, illuminating its potential strengths and pitfalls. Although their essay applies to all service-learning, they also explore its ramifications for peace studies.

The second set of essays discuss peace studies programs that incorporate SL. Although most deal with undergraduate programs (and here, more often than not they offer either minors or certificates rather than majors), two essays focus on graduate opportunities. Some of the programs have a central office that facilitates SL placements, while others do not. Some rely exclusively on SL placements in nearby communities; others offer students international placements as well. Although some of the programs are rooted in religious traditions, others draw sustenance from the democratic tradition of citizen involvement.

Marullo, Lance, and Schwarz discuss the importance of the Catholic and Jesuit traditions at Georgetown University for the identity and (politically important) acceptance of the Justice and Peace program there; the program integrates community service via volunteer service or SL placements facilitated by the Volunteer and Public Service Center. The Justice and Peace Studies program at the University of St. Thomas, as presented by Smith and Haasl, also has roots in the Catholic tradition and emphasizes, in particular, work with people on the margins; the program is structured around a four-stage "circle of praxis." As Roschelle, Turpin, and Elias discuss, Peace and Justice Studies at the University of San Francisco was designed as a special fit with the Jesuit mission of social justice. It requires SL in one of the fieldwork courses as well as in one of the elective courses, both of which are aimed at providing opportunities to understand the larger societal context and the potential students have for promoting positive social change in it. Earlham College offers students an opportunity in Northern Ireland, as explained by

Bing, to experience and better understand their own attitudes and approaches as they learn about and make their contribution to the processes of peace in communities divided by conflict. The International and National Voluntary Service Training (INVST) program at the University of Colorado at Boulder, as Scarritt and Lowe discuss, is a two-year SL leadership training program that seeks to prepare students to analyze and work for solutions to community problems. From wilderness experiences to work with the Dineh Nation to placements in Jamaica, the program offers students theory- and skill-based opportunities to prepare them for lifelong active roles in their communities.

We present two programs at the graduate level. The Applied Practice and Theory program for graduate students at the Institute for Conflict Analysis and Resolution (ICAR) at George Mason University, as Blechman describes it, offers students SL opportunities to work in teams in situations of conflict-divided societies, communities, or schools. Using a case study with the "schools" team, Blechman points to what makes the nitty-gritty aspects of the SL so frustrating, challenging, and, in the long run, worthwhile in such settings. Walsh and Garner discuss the new M.A. in International Service at Roehampton Institute, a program that is based on a four-institution, three-country collaboration. It incorporates SL in international settings, followed by SL in London, and focuses on students' obligations to "develop and demonstrate responsibility for their own learning."

From SL in programs we move to SL in particular courses. The essays provide details on SL placements, the amount of service, the range of assignments, issues of grading, and outcomes of such placements. Crews begins with a discussion of his Introduction to Peace and Conflict Studies, in which SL is an option for students and selection of sites is enhanced because of a community-wide database of participating agencies. Also discussing an introductory course, Merrill articulates her rationale for incorporating SL, with an emphasis on issues of stereotyping, crossing cultures, and the centrality of identities in conflict situations. James-Deramo examines an interdisciplinary faith-justice course, Hunger for Justice, in which a well-structured syllabus and plan for the course runs head-on into the reality of few students and what adaptations a faculty must make in light of that reality check. Richards and Schwendener-Holt describe a methods course in which the rationale for SL is rooted in the theories of Paulo Freire and Antonio Gramsci and the focus on social change is central. In a discussion of Introduction to Cultural Geography, Kimsey focuses on the key concept of culture and examines how SL placements can advance students' understanding of the uniqueness and universality of cultures while affording them opportunities to serve in and with different ethnic groups. Finally, MacDougall provides an example of an assignment that should encourage faculty to get involved. His "mini-internship" assignment, while straddling the traditional separation between internships and SL, offers a concrete way for faculty to explore the potential of service-learning in peace studies.

We hope that with this volume those interested in the intersection of peace studies and service-learning will find theoretical as well as practical help on how to proceed. The challenges are real, and the work is time intensive. But we believe that those who choose to enter this domain will find the process enlivening and, ultimately, a real contribution to "teaching for justice."

Notes

1. See Crews's first essay in this volume for an alternative conceptualization.

2. See Weigert's essay in this volume for a discussion of EL and SL.

References

Ackerman, Peter, and Christopher Kruegler. (1993). *Strategic Nonviolent Conflict: The Dynamics of People Power in the Twentieth Century*. Westport, CT: Praeger.

Bing, Anthony G. (July 1989). "Peace Studies as Experiential Education." *The Annals of the American Academy of Political and Social Science* 504: 48-60.

Bondurant, Joan V. (1965, orig. 1958). *Conquest of Violence: The Gandhian Philosophy of Conflict*. Berkeley, CA: University of California Press.

Boulding, Elise. (1990, orig. 1988). *Building a Global Civic Culture: Education for an Interdependent World*. Syracuse, NY: Syracuse University Press.

Brock-Utne, Birgit. (1985). *Educating for Peace: A Feminist Perspective*. Elmsford, NY: Pergamon Press.

Carter, April. (1992). *Peace Movements: International Protest and World Politics Since 1945*. London: Longman.

DeBenedetti, Charles, ed. (1986). *Peace Heroes in Twentieth-Century America*. Bloomington, IN: Indiana University Press.

Galtung, Johan. (1964). "An Editorial." *Journal of Peace Research* 1(1): 1-4.

Giles, Jr., Dwight E., and Janet Eyler. (1998). "A Service Learning Research Agenda for the Next Five Years." In *Academic Service Learning: A Pedagogy of Action and Reflection*, edited by R. Rhoads and J. Howard, pp. 65-72. San Francisco, CA: Jossey-Bass.

Harris, Ian M., issue ed. (1996). "Peace Education in a Postmodern World." *Peabody Journal of Education* 71(3).

Hicks, David, ed. (1988). *Education for Peace: Issues, Principles, and Practice in the Classroom.* London: Routledge.

Lakey, George. (1987). *Powerful Peacemaking: A Strategy for a Living Revolution.* Philadelphia, PA: New Society Publishers.

Lantieri, Linda, and Janet Patti. (1996). *Waging Peace in Our Schools.* Boston, MA: Beacon Press.

Lopez, George, special ed. (July 1989). "Peace Studies: Past and Future." *The Annals of the American Academy of Political and Social Science* 504.

McGillis, Daniel. (1997). *Community Mediation Programs: Developments and Challenges.* Washington, DC: U.S. Department of Justice.

Melchior, Alan. (1998). *National Evaluation of Learn and Serve America School and Community-Based Programs: Final Report.* Waltham, MA: Center for Human Resources, Brandeis University.

Nyden, Philip, Anne Figert, Mark Shibley, and Darryl Burrows. (1997). *Building Community: Social Science in Action.* Thousands Oaks, CA: Pine Forge Press.

Powers, Roger, and William H. Vogele, eds. (1997). *Protest, Power, and Change: An Encyclopedia of Nonviolent Action From Act-Up to Women's Suffrage.* New York, NY: Garland.

Reardon, Betty A. (1988). *Comprehensive Peace Education: Educating for Global Responsibility.* New York, NY: Teachers College, Columbia University.

Salla, Michael, Walter Tonetto, and Enrique Martinez, eds. (1995). *Essays on Peace: Paradigms for Global Order.* Rockhampton, Queensland: Central Queensland University Press.

Saltmarsh, John. (Summer 1998). "Exploring the Meanings of Community-University Partnerships." *NSEE Quarterly* 23(4): 6-7, 21-22.

Schwerin, Edward W. (1995). *Mediation, Citizen Power, and Transformational Politics.* Westport, CT: Praeger.

Sharp, Gene. (1973). *The Politics of Nonviolent Action.* 3 vols. Boston, MA: Porter Sargent.

———. (1990). *Civilian-Based Defense: A Post-Military Weapons System.* Princeton, NJ: Princeton University Press.

Weigert, Kathleen Maas. (July 1989). "Peace Studies as Education for Nonviolent Social Change." *The Annals of the American Academy of Political and Social Science* 504: 37-47.

———. (July 1990). "Experiential Learning and Peace Education: On Visiting Greenham Common Women's Peace Camp." *Peace and Change* 15(3): 312-330.

Whyte, William Foote. (1991). *Participatory Action Research.* Newbury Park, CA: Sage.

Moral Dimensions of Peace Studies:
A Case for Service-Learning

by Kathleen Maas Weigert

In the post-Cold War world of the late 20th century, in which old theories seem inadequate to the emerging realities around the globe, the challenges to peace studies are powerful. One challenge revolves around the issue of preparing students for their participation in creating that new world. What are the critical skills they need to learn for a realistic yet imaginative understanding of the global situation and the local-global nexus? Will they choose to get involved and see as both duty and delight the responsibility for helping to create a more just and peace-filled world? It is the purpose of this essay to argue that the pedagogy of experiential learning (EL) in general and service-learning (SL) in particular is a powerful vehicle for enhancing knowledge about peace and violence in our contemporary world and developing ideas, motivations, and skills for action in the struggle to make this world a better one. In presenting this case, I frame the essay around three concepts — the moral realm, peace, and education — and I conclude with seven statements based on the analysis. I hope the reader will be persuaded about the importance of EL and SL for peace studies. I hasten to add that while I am making the case for the inclusion of SL in peace studies, I am not suggesting that this case cannot be made for other fields; in fact, I would submit the contrary. But it is up to scholars in the other fields to make that argument. My argument is simple: SL has the potential for combining, in a compelling and enlivening way, the concern peace educators have for contributing to students' understanding of peace as well as to their desire to lead a good life, with the aim of enhancing students' commitment to doing their part, in collaboration with others, in the struggle to effect a more just and peace-filled world.

The Moral Realm

It is with a bit of trepidation that I begin with the conceptual terrain of the moral realm. Although the term *moral* is perhaps most often viewed as "belonging" to the province of philosophers and theologians, I am neither; my formal training is in international relations and sociology. Yet, I think all people benefit by refusing to give up an ordinary, everyday sense of the term rather than placing it primarily (if not exclusively) in the hands of experts. The dialogue Robert Coles had with one of his students comes to mind. She asked him an "unnerving question": "What's the point of *knowing* good, if you don't keep trying to *become* a good person?" (1995, italics in original). That is a fair question; it is also an eminently important one, and it is in that ordinary, unsophisticated sense of doing "good" and becoming "good" that I place my discussion of the term *moral* and urge its centrality to the goals of peace studies. What are we trying to do as teachers (and, I would contend, as researchers, as well) in peace studies?

Let us start with dictionary definitions of *moral. The American Heritage Dictionary of the English Language* (Morris 1980) offers the following two definitions: "of or concerned with the judgment of the goodness or badness of human action and character; pertaining to the discernment of good and evil" and "designed to teach goodness or correctness of character and behavior; instructive of what is good and bad." My first formal encounter with the moral realm came in an undergraduate course in which we read Aristotle's *Nichomachean Ethics* (McKeon 1947). I learned at least two important things from that experience. First, that the "good" is the aim of any action, and that the end of politics is the good for humans (or for "man," as Aristotle put it). Second, that there is a difference in the learning processes for acquiring intellectual and moral virtues. Although the former are developed initially through teaching, the latter are formed by habit or practice. In other words, we acquire moral virtues by first putting them into action; we become "just," for example, by the practice of just actions. The concern is to develop the habits of a life that is "good" or that contribute to the "good."

Now these actions and pursuit of the good do not take place in a vacuum. As I mentioned above, I am a sociologist, so it will not be surprising that I start with the idea that, since we are social animals, the pursuit of the good takes place in the context of some larger social grouping. While fraught with difficulty, the term *community* captures one notion. We are members from birth of some kind of community, which socializes us into its culture, its norms and mores. This socialization has a cognitive and an affective dimension. We learn not only what ideas to think but also what emotions to feel in which circumstances. We learn to feel revulsion or delight, for example, at eating certain kinds of food or participating in certain kinds of rituals. We learn more generally what constitutes a good life and what the common good is. Cultural anthropologists have helped us appreciate the great diversity of human communities in this regard. Thus, we know there is indeed no one version of the "good life." Nevertheless, at least in our early childhood years, we are socialized into our own culture's (or subculture's) vision of that good life.

Central to the socialization process is the institution of education, both formal and informal. And within this broadly conceived educational domain, we find the importance of such "transmitters" of the culture as stories and particular behaviors in the shaping of each generation. Key to both is the skill of imagination — a point to which I return below (see Boulding 1990 and Rivage-Seul 1987). Stories provide role models: cautionary tales if they are about those who do not subscribe to the mores of the culture and find themselves considered "deviants" with the concomitant loss of resources; hortatory ones if they are instead about people who seem to embody those mores and are rewarded accordingly. The interest in stories about those trying to lead good lives finds a contemporary outlet in the works of such authors as Colby and Damon (1992), Coles (1993), and Daloz et al. (1996). The concern with actions as ways of engendering certain values and skills can be found as well in the service-learning movement, to which I return in a later section.

A final point to note is that as we mature, if we have been given the tools and/or the experiences, we come to examine our cultural stories and actions from a comparative perspective and with a critical eye, asking such pivotal questions as: Is this how I and others would define a "good life"? How can I work with others in seeking to live a good life? What are the best ways to achieve and live out the good life I seek? It seems to me that these very moral questions are central to the peace studies project. This leads to the second term, *peace*.

Peace: Definitions and Dimensions

The field of peace studies is fairly new as an academic offering in higher education. Manchester College in Indiana is said to have been the first to offer peace studies when it initiated its program in 1948. This is an inter-, multi-, and transdisciplinary field that addresses issues involved in the processes and structures of building peace and reducing violence (see Barash 1991; Burton 1997; Elias and Turpin 1994; Klare 1994; Turpin and Kurtz 1997; Wehr et al. 1994). It seems simplest to say that the field focuses on the concepts of peace, conflict, nonviolence, and violence (war in particular). If one is looking for consensus on the key terms, disappointment will result; the terms are rich and contested. Galtung (1969) gave salience to the distinction between "negative" and "positive" peace by separating out types of violence, using the term *negative peace* to refer to the absence of war and "direct" violence, and the term *positive peace* to refer to the absence of "structural violence," or, to put it affirmatively, the presence of social justice (see Weigert forthcoming). Recently, Crews (1999) has suggested using the terms *essential peace* and *shadows of peace*.

However defined, peace is a complex idea that needs to be reexamined with each generation and that calls for contributions from all interested in conceptualizing and effecting it in the multiple levels of everyday life. In the

Cold War era, for example, many political leaders and scholars thought it sufficient to consider peace as something secured by deterrence, while the world situation today demands a much more inclusive notion. Another example: The "environment" is no longer just the background to human actions; it is seen as the home to humans and many other species whose very lives depend on how humans interact with it. The "global community" and the "global common good" are concepts that cannot be dismissed out of hand as muddled notions of soft-headed activists.

It also seems fair to say that, at least for many who teach this subject matter, peace studies can be seen as an applied branch of knowledge. Like health sciences, peace studies is not "value free" but rather "in favor of" peace over violence, at a minimum, and at the fullest, in favor of such values as justice, equality, basic needs being met, and so forth. The goal is to better understand peace and violence so that people can collaborate in constructing a better world. While peace studies is not therefore "neutral," it does purport to be "objective," in that its practitioners seek to examine fairly all views, to take into account all relevant variables, and to uphold high standards of intersubjective evidence (Barash 1991: 26). Thus, it is highly relevant — indeed, some might argue it is essential — to instructors of peace studies to consider how the subject matter relates to ideas and actions that people, as individuals and as members of various communities, can have and can take in their immediate surroundings, in career choices, in being citizens. Although there may not be universal agreement about the particular kinds of action people take, that people act nonviolently, as much as possible, is a strong value.

A Perspective on Education

I enter another domain often conceived of as belonging to a group of specialists, and I make the same disclaimer; while not trained in the field of education, I want to employ the key concept in an ordinary usage context. Here I begin with another dictionary formulation, using in this case the *Oxford English Dictionary* (OED). The OED notes that *education* has its roots in two words: *educare*, meaning "to rear or to bring forth," and *educere*, meaning "to lead forth." One of the definitions the OED offers is "to train (any person) so as to develop the intellectual and moral powers generally." Quite clearly we are led back to Aristotle and the moral realm. We can go back further to Plato's teacher, Socrates, whose dictum in *The Apology* (Rouse 1956: 443) has become a mantra for some: "the greatest good for a man [sic] every day [is] to discuss virtue . . . and that life without inquiry is not worth living."

So, in this line of thinking, we can properly conceive of education as a process that has to do with knowing, desiring, and doing the good. Teachers of peace studies are indeed interested in the development of their students' intellectual and moral powers so that the students can be better equipped to pursue and create knowledge, reflect on it, and incorporate it into leading a good life. I hasten to add, education is decidedly different from indoctrination, which has as its core the attempt to negate independence of thought and reflective action, and instead to elicit acquiescence with some dogma and conformity in some behavior. Like any in the academy, peace studies teachers strive to be pedagogues, not ideologues.

Redefining Roles and Concepts

But what about the "intellectual powers" referred to in the definition above? It is here that several writers have been instrumental in my own thinking: Paulo Freire, Parker Palmer, and bell hooks. Let me suggest kernels of their thought that have been fruitful for me in thinking about peace studies.

The late Paulo Freire (1993, orig. 1970) helped in relating the idea of being "oppressed" to the ways in which people are taught; notions of authority and power become central. I learned two critical ideas from him. The first is the distinction between the "banking model" of education and the "problem-posing" model. What I found so helpful, because it resonated with my experience both as a teacher and as a student, is the idea that the student is not an empty vessel into which the authority pours knowledge to be retrieved at some future time under conditions set by the authority. Instead, the student is an active person, and the authority, if true to the call of teaching, helps in setting up an environment so that the student can indeed grapple with ideas, their "truthfulness" in the context of the student's life, and their possibility for liberating the self in those circumstances.

The second idea is Freire's insight into the roles of teacher and student, the former now conceived as "teacher-as-student" and the latter as "student-as-teacher." The idea that is basic to both of these Freirean contributions is that each person has something to offer others, each something to receive, and the community is better off in the process and in the product(s) that emerge. This alters the learning context in ways that emphasize the responsibility of the individual and of the community as a whole to be active participants in the education process.

This leads to Parker Palmer's contribution. The title of one of his books points to his perspective: *To Know as We Are Known: A Spirituality of Education* (1993). He offers this as a conceptualization of teaching: "To teach is to create a space in which the community of truth is practiced" (xii). What does that mean? First of all, it suggests in part what Freire has urged: We need to change the context, the roles, the space or place in which education is offered, so that it is supportive and encouraging of growth. Second, it means that each has something to offer, and no one's offering can be dismissed out of hand. Third, it means each takes seriously the obligation to work. It is only under these conditions that the very idea of "truth" can be pursued, let alone "practiced." Fourth, it affirms the importance of the community, "a rich and complex network of relationships in which we must both speak and listen, make claims on others, and make ourselves accountable" (xii).

Speaking of practices leads directly to bell hooks. The title of her 1994 work provides insight into what she offers: *Teaching to Transgress: Education as the Practice of Freedom.* For hooks, "borders" become central; willingness to reconceive authority roles is pivotal; creating an environment in which individuals can risk is imperative. Like Aristotle, hooks affirms the crucial place of "practicing" freedom, of growing, of taking risks. If the teacher assumes the role of "the authority" and squelches the voices of the students, the teacher has, in this view, abused power. "Authority of experience" comes into play here. Although it is a term that can sometimes lead to stifling others, if the learning environment is well constructed and faithfully (consistently) paid attention to, the authority of experience of each person can be acknowledged, and teacher and students alike can make contributions to the practice of freedom. Like Palmer, hooks also uses the term *community*, especially in the phrase "learning community," a communal context for learning. We can choose to help "create" such a community. And it seems to me, it is in such communities, building on (and in some case, yes, rejecting) what we learned first in the family or school or neighborhood community, that the moral education that is key to the fully human life can take place.

How does this happen? Centrally through conversation. It is not without reason that the "Great Books," for example, have been called the "great conversation." We converse with our contemporaries in the classroom setting and "with" our ancestors in the discussion of their works. If those works are to be more than museum pieces, we question them, disagree with them, extend them, and appropriate what is meaningful for our own lives, keeping them "alive" in that way and "continuing" the conversation. So it is with whatever works we employ as peace studies teachers; each of us reads them and then we come together in our learning community to explore their meanings, to "converse" about how they relate to our lives and work.

"Action" in Education

But conversation in the classroom is not the only way. A second way, which can be employed within as well as outside of the classroom context, is a kind of practice or action. The pedagogy under which this can be examined is typically labeled "experiential learning," meaning "hands-on learning" or "learning activities that engage the learner directly in the phenomena being studied" (Kendall et al. 1986: 1). Experiential learning has a long and vibrant history. Although not all practitioners would agree on a list of "core ingredients" (anymore than peace studies scholars agree on such a list), it seems safe to say that most believe there is a difference, for example, between the lecture format and experiential learning. In the former, the role of the teacher is to be the authority, the one in control of the classroom, the one responsible for communicating knowledge (sometimes in a question-answer format) and for assessing whether the students have learned the material. The role of the student is to attend the lectures, to listen well, to read carefully, to take notes, to study those notes, and to demonstrate mastery of the material when asked by the teacher. Surely there are excellent lectures, and surely learning can and does take place in such a context — those are not the issues.

The issues instead revolve around the roles of teacher and student. Take the ideas of control and responsibility. In experiential learning, the student has more control of and greater responsibility for the learning process than in the more typical classroom situation. It is also clear that the physicality of the individual is differently involved. In the standard classroom, students sit in designated places and the teacher is at the "front" of the room. In experiential learning classes, people move around; there is no "one center," no "one authority." Experiential learning can take numerous forms, some inside the classroom (such as role-playing exercises and student-led discussions) and some in other settings (such as internships and laboratory experiments).

Two additional groups of scholars and scholar-activists have contributed to my understanding of the place action can have in education. Feminists have made two key contributions in this arena. First, it was from feminists that I initially encountered the critique of the traditional distinctions between public and private life and between objective and subjective. Brock-Utne (1989), building on earlier works of Galtung and others, included in her theorizing the idea that the concept of negative peace had to include the absence of collective, personal violence against women, in effect, incorporating what many had considered a "private" issue into a very public category for theoretical and empirical analysis. Second and related, feminists (as well as other analysts) helped enlarge the concept of power, moving it from the traditional, vertical understanding of "power over" some (to make them do what the power-holder wants) to the more horizontal idea of "power to" or "power with," unleashing the idea of capacity for those who for so long were both theoretically and empirically considered bereft of power. In short, "ordinary" people can work together to effect change. Lappé and DuBois (1994: 47), for example, define power as "the capacity to act publicly and effectively, to bring about positive change, to build hope."

The second group of scholars, "nonviolentists" as Holmes (1990) calls them, have helped people learn about effective nonviolent ways of bringing about change, from the intrapersonal to the global. Two of the classics in this area are Richard Gregg's work *The Power of Nonviolence* (1959) and the three-volume work by Gene Sharp *The Politics of Nonviolent Action* (1973). The word *nonviolence* is rich and, like *peace*, heavily contested. One perspective is to conceive of violence-nonviolence as a continuum on which the polar points are differentiated on the criterion of the extent of the refusal to use physical force and/or psychological harm to achieve one's personal and/or societal goals. One way in which feminist thought joins with nonviolent thought is through the extension of what Ruddick (1989) conceives to be the "maternal practices" (i.e., preservation, growth, and social acceptability in raising children) to a larger societal plane of dealing with other societies, nation-states, and so forth.

Service-Learning

This leads to a consideration of the particular kind of experiential learning called service-learning. Let us begin again with the term itself, prefaced by the recurring theme: This concept is rich and enthusiastically debated. A number of works, including the whole of this AAHE series, help elucidate the history and use of the term (see Jacoby 1996 and Kendall 1990). Some suggest the term *community learning* for this pedagogy (Seidel and Zlotkowski 1993). I have found it fruitful to substitute the term *community-based learning* for this pedagogy, because it seems to incorporate some of the good envisioned in the SL vocabulary while avoiding some of the difficulties; for example, the idea that "service" connotes noblesse oblige or that service is a one-way relationship (see Weigert 1998). But no matter what term is preferred, there is again a generally agreed-upon set of ideas that characterizes what is involved. I believe one way to capture these ideas is by three R's: roles, reciprocity, and reflection.

Roles: Using the term in the sociological sense of expected behavior and attitudes appropriate to a status or position, there are at least four key roles in a simple model of SL. One has to do with the official teacher of the course. The role of the teacher in SL is to examine the course goals to determine whether any of the goals can be well met by an SL assignment and, if the answer is yes, to find the appropriate site(s) for student service; to work out an agreement with the appropriate community representatives about the nature and length of that service; to prepare the students for the service; and to establish the criteria for evaluating and assessing the service in light of the course goals. (Of course, all of this is greatly facilitated if the college or university has an office for service-learning.) For the peace studies teacher, this is the opportunity to make concrete the link between "teaching about" and "teaching for" peace and the difficulties embedded in both. An SL opportunity at a women's refuge can provide the student with the opportunity to ponder the links between direct and indirect violence; an opportunity at a shelter for homeless people can raise the challenges of building positive peace; one with a local chapter of the War Resister's League or the United Nations Association can elicit the thorny issues involved in building movements aimed at bringing about nonviolent social change. Such SL assignments call forth the imagination needed to envision a better world and to make concrete various ways of effecting it.

A second role relates to the student whose obligation is to enter into the service with the necessary skills and attitudes to begin the work, to faithfully and creatively perform the service for the stipulated amount of time, to "learn" (in the fullest, most critical, and imaginative sense of the term) from the experience, and to demonstrate the learning that is related to the course material and goals. A third role is that of the representative of the agency or community group or service site. This person's role is to help faculty understand the nature of the agency and to assist faculty in selecting the appropriate service opportunities at the site in light of the course goals, to "monitor" the students' service work, and to participate in some way in assessing and evaluating the students' service. A final role, in which SL involves a specific individual who is considered the "recipient" of some direct service, relates to that recipient. He or she must have some control (which varies, of course, with age, abilities, and the like) over the nature, context, and duration of the service requested.

Reciprocity: Implicit in the preceding paragraph is the idea that all the actors contribute to the process. There are various levels of interaction and involvement in SL. There are relationships between campus and community, sustained through a partnership or a collaborative model, at the heart of this pedagogy (Gugerty and Swezey 1996). There is the teacher-student relationship (and here I would hearken back to the ideas from Freire, Palmer, and hooks), as well as that between student and recipient of service. Respect is essential on the part of all. Each must understand what the others contribute so that accountability may be assured, difficulties attended to in a forthright manner, exploitation avoided, and progress toward goals evaluated impartially. In the best case, all reciprocally teach and learn, as those terms are used in this essay.

Reflection: Using the term, for the moment, in the sense of "to throw back, to think or consider seriously," we can assert that reflection is essential for each of the actors in SL, not just for students — and not just at one point in time (see Eyler et al. 1996, Goldsmith 1995, and Reed and Koliba n.d.). Students are often first thought of when the issue of reflection is raised. Most assuredly they must do reflection on a regular basis in order to learn from their service work. Reflection must come in the context of the class, through required assignments of some kind (e.g., journal-writing assignments, discussions, oral presentations, and the like). Not all student reflection needs to be highly structured, but all of it does call for some element of guidance in the context of the course.

In deciding to incorporate an SL assignment, a teacher must of necessity begin the planning process by determining what issues are involved in the various course goals and how an SL assignment might address them. As students reflect on what they are encountering and learning from the service work (in oral or written form), their instructor (who has, most likely, designed the reflection assignments) is called upon to participate in that process, to challenge and support the linking of service to course goals, to critically evaluate how the service is or is not contributing to the goals, and to reflect on what is not going well and why, etc. And at the end of the course, the teacher is called upon for the culminating reflection questions: How fruitful was this assignment for the course as I envisioned it? What might I do differently next time?

Site or agency representatives, whose jobs are not often characterized by frequent opportunities to participate in set times of reflection, will nevertheless employ certain mechanisms to ensure that some time is given to reflecting on the students' service work, on how well she or he is monitoring that work, and on the students' contributions to the recipients of the service as well as to the overall work of the agency. Finally, where there is a direct recipient of the service; that person needs to be given opportunities to reflect on the service provided, on his or her attitudes and behavior, and on the progress toward established goals.

It is the combination of careful attention to the roles, to the issues of reciprocity, and to the opportunities for reflection that makes service-learning such a potentially powerful vehicle for the practice of peace in the context of education.

Conclusions

Weaving together the implicit and explicit ideas presented above, I want to state the case for the importance of service-learning in peace studies. First, one purpose of education is to create and share knowledge in order to lead a good life. Second, a good life, in its communal and societal aspects, is one that manifests concern for the well-being of others and commitment to the universal common good. Third, the role of the teacher is to help create an environment that will contribute to the development of intellectual and moral strengths, which in turn assists the student in leading a good life. Fourth, peace studies is a field that focuses in particular on the analytical and empirical relationships between peace and nonviolence in the search for a good life. Fifth, the common good can be advanced through nonviolent means that can be learned and that must be practiced inside and outside the classroom. Sixth, one rich pedagogy for such practice is experiential learning in general and service-learning in particular. Seventh, the formal "teacher" of peace studies should provide opportunities for such learning; the formal "students" must demand them if they are not offered.

References

Barash, David P. (1991). *Introduction to Peace Studies*. Belmont, CA: Wadsworth.

Boulding, Elise. (1990, orig. 1988). *Building a Global Civic Culture: Education for an Interdependent World*. Syracuse, NY: Syracuse University Press.

Brock-Utne, Birgit. (1989). *Feminist Perspectives on Peace and Peace Education*. Elmsford, NY: Pergamon Press.

Burton, John W. (1997). *Violence Explained: The Sources of Conflict, Violence and Crime and Their Provention*. Manchester and New York, NY: Manchester University Press.

Colby, Anne, and William Damon. (1992). *Some Do Care: Contemporary Lives of Moral Commitment*. New York, NY: The Free Press.

Coles, Robert. (1993). *The Call of Service: A Witness to Idealism*. Boston, MA: Houghton Mifflin.

————— . (September 22, 1995). "The Disparity Between Intellect and Character." *The Chronicle of Higher Education* 42: A68.

Crews, Robin. (1999). "Peace." In *The Oxford Companion to American Military History*, edited by John Whiteclay Chambers II. New York, NY: Oxford University Press.

Daloz, Laurent A., Cheryl H. Keen, James P. Keen, and Sharon D. Parks. (1996). *Common Fire: Lives of Commitment in a Complex World*. Boston, MA: Beacon Press.

Elias, Robert, and Jennifer Turpin, eds. (1994). *Rethinking Peace*. Boulder, CO: Lynne Rienner.

Eyler, Janet, Dwight E. Giles, Jr., and Angela Schmiede. (1996). *A Practitioner's Guide to Reflection in Service-Learning: Student Voices and Reflections*. Nashville, TN: Vanderbilt University.

Freire, Paulo. (1993, orig. 1970). *Pedagogy of the Oppressed, New Revised 20th-Anniversary Edition*. New York, NY: Continuum.

Galtung, Johan. (1969). "Violence, Peace, and Peace Research." *Journal of Peace Research* 6(3): 167-191.

Goldsmith, Suzanne. (1995). *Journal Reflection: A Resource Guide for Community Service Leaders and Educators Engaged in Service Learning*. Washington, DC: The American Alliance for Rights & Responsibilities.

Gregg, Richard B. (1959, orig. 1935). *The Power of Nonviolence*. Nyack, NY: Fellowship Publications.

Gugerty, Catherine R., and Erin D. Swezey. (1996). "Developing Campus-Community Relationships." In *Service-Learning in Higher Education: Concepts and Practices*, edited by Barbara Jacoby and Associates, pp. 92-108. San Francisco, CA: Jossey-Bass.

Holmes, Robert L. (1990). "General Introduction." In *Nonviolence in Theory and Practice*, edited by Robert L. Holmes, pp. 1-6. Belmont, CA: Wadsworth.

hooks, bell. (1994). *Teaching to Transgress: Education as the Practice of Freedom*. New York, NY: Routledge.

Jacoby, Barbara. (1996). "Service-Learning in Today's Higher Education." In *Service-Learning in Higher Education: Concepts and Practices*, edited by Barbara Jacoby and Associates, pp. 3-25. San Francisco, CA: Jossey-Bass.

Kendall, Jane C., ed. (1990). *Combining Service and Learning: A Resource Book for Community and Public Service. Vol. 1*. Raleigh, NC: National Society for Experiential Education.

Kendall, J., and Associates. (1986). *Strengthening Experiential Education Within Your Institution*. Raleigh, NC: National Society for Internships and Experiential Education.

Klare, Michael T., ed. (1994). *Peace and World Security Studies: A Curriculum Guide, 6th Edition*. Boulder, CO: Lynne Rienner.

Lappé, Frances Moore, and Paul Martin DuBois. (1994). *The Quickening of America: Rebuilding Our Nation, Remaking Our Lives*. San Francisco, CA: Jossey-Bass.

McKeon, Richard, ed. (1947). *Introduction to Aristotle*. New York, NY: The Modern Library, Random House.

Morris, William. (1980). *The American Heritage Dictionary of the English Language*. Boston, MA: Houghton Mifflin.

Palmer, Parker. (1993, orig. 1983). *To Know as We Are Known: A Spirituality of Education*. San Francisco, CA: Harper and Row.

Reed, Julie, and Christopher Koliba. (n.d.). *Facilitating Reflection: A Manual for Higher Education*. Washington, DC: Georgetown University, Volunteer and Public Service Center.

Rivage-Seul, Marguerite K. (May 1987). "Peace Education: Moral Imagination and the Pedagogy of the Oppressed." *Harvard Educational Review* 57(2): 153-169.

Rouse, W.H.D., trans. (1956). *Great Dialogues of Plato*. New York, NY: The New American Library.

Ruddick, Sarah. (1989). *Maternal Thinking: Toward a Politics of Peace*. Boston, MA: Beacon Press.

Sharp, Gene. (1973). *The Politics of Nonviolent Action*. 3 vols. Boston, MA: Porter Sargent.

Seidel, Robert, and Edward Zlotkowski. (May-June 1993). "Common Ground: From Service-Learning to Community-Learning." *Experiential Education* 18(3): 10, 15.

Turpin, Jennifer, and Lester R. Kurtz, eds. (1997). *The Web of Violence: From Interpersonal to Global.* Urbana, IL: University of Illinois.

Wehr, Paul, Heidi Burgess, and Guy Burgess, eds. (1994). *Justice Without Violence.* Boulder, CO, and London: Lynne Rienner.

Weigert, Kathleen Maas. (1998). "Academic Service Learning: Its Meaning and Relevance." In *Academic Service Learning: A Pedagogy of Action and Reflection,* edited by R. Rhoads and J. Howard, pp. 3-10. San Francisco, CA: Jossey-Bass.

————. (Forthcoming). "Structural Violence." In *Encyclopedia of Violence, Peace and Conflict,* edited by Lester R. Kurtz. San Diego, CA: Academic Press.

Peace Studies, Pedagogy, and Social Change

by Robin J. Crews

When we started this book on service-learning within peace studies courses and programs, we knew we could not expect most readers to have a working knowledge of both peace studies and service-learning. Thus, one objective all along has been the dual agenda of introducing peace studies faculty to service-learning pedagogies *and* service-learning practitioners to the academic field of peace studies. Since this book is neither a treatise on peace studies nor a primer on service-learning, we may achieve these dual purposes only indirectly at best.

One of the salient strengths that peace studies and service-learning have in common is the extent to which they *humanize* and *personalize* learning (a theme to which I will return later). What this essay attempts to do is approach our larger objective diagonally and, it is hoped, in ways that benefit from, and embody, the "human" and "personal" dimensions of peace studies and service-learning. In other words, this narrative is an analytical reflection about my own journey through peace studies into service-learning.

Peace Studies as Prologue

During and after my undergraduate years, I found myself engaged in a passionate search for a viable way to connect conscience, education, and action. Wherever I looked, I could see the need for constructive social change. I saw violence all around me (direct and indirect, intentional and unintentional, psychological and physical, toward others and toward nature) and did not understand how we were capable of it, where it came from, or how to get beyond it.

Some six years out of college, I found myself in graduate school pursuing peace studies, wanting to learn as much as I could about the causes of violence and the ways in which we could learn about peaceful means of coexisting with one another. What I rediscovered with every book I read and course I took is that violence, for the most part, is learned. As is nonviolence.

Thus, the path I sought (education) necessarily involved social change through learning. Instead of adopting a safe track and keeping the status quo humming an equilibrial tune, I decided to take my first steps toward envisioning different futures that would include, among other things, a world without violence. Although I certainly wanted to help those around me who were suffering from violence right then, I also knew that I could do that forever, while the underlying causes (e.g., values, belief systems, and ideologies; fear; violent rituals and traditions; violent behavior and experience) that produced structural violence (e.g., hunger, poverty, discrimination, exploitation) would continue to outpace me and others like me — and produce increasing numbers of victims.

Of course, it is crucial to attend to both immediate and long-term agendas: I would never advocate that we look the other way when violence hurts those around us in the present. But if we limit ourselves solely to treating symptoms in the present moment, we never will address the larger, structural causes of those symptoms. If we do not focus on the future, we remain in reactive problem-solving modes concerned with symptoms, instead of embracing proactive modes that can transform structural causes. What I have had the opportunity to learn since the mid-1970s, however, is that constructive social change of this kind is a most ambitious goal.

Transforming Academia in Order to Transform Society

This decision created an entirely new set of agendas and questions for me involving the need for social change within academia. How does one attempt to contribute to larger social change when the vehicle one employs to accomplish this is itself in need of repair? To make matters even more challenging, I was pursuing social change from within a relatively new, transdisciplinary field of study that (1) was located near the bottom of various discipline-based hierarchies in academia; (2) along with sociology and other social sciences, included social institutions, e.g., academia, as legitimate objects of analysis; and (3) sought modest improvements in them.

In general, pursuit of these goals has engendered significant amounts of creativity, self-reflection, and questioning, on the one hand, and limited success, on the other. However, despite many obstacles, peace studies (including conflict resolution) did make substantive advances during the last two decades of the Cold War. Peace studies programs developed on hundreds of college and university campuses; several national and international organizations came into being to serve as venues for networking, discussing and advancing theory, pedagogy, and curriculum development; the literature grew; and the number of courses on peace, justice, conflict resolution, world order studies, security studies (and violent conflict and war) grew as well. And more foundations started supporting the field in small ways.

The Failures of War and "Negative Peace"

What happened to peace studies at the end of the Cold War is the best indication yet that our own field had had insufficient impact on academia, let alone the world. From foundations to deans to chancellors, what we heard was that, with the end of the Cold War, we had finally arrived at "peace"; thus, there was no longer a pressing need to support peace studies. At the time, this discourse about and within peace studies derived from a larger dialogue on national security, war, and "peace" that assumed that peace was, simply, the absence of war. This way of thinking about peace is not confined to the past: it continues to be a (perhaps *the*) dominant image of peace in the West. Such conclusions (i.e., that peace is the absence of war, and that with the end of one war, peace studies is no longer needed) invite us to engage in a serious assessment of our progress and future goals within academia and society at large.

As a result of the relationship between national security, defense, and higher education, the end of the Cold War also gave rise to a reassessment of the perceived "fat" within our colleges, universities, and research institutions, as well as the role of higher education in society. After all, if we had no ideological enemy anymore and no major wars left to fight, why did we need all those expensive universities? One outcome was a reactionary downsizing of financial support for education. The resulting political and economic dynamics amplified existing pressures on young, interdisciplinary fields of study within academia in the United States, and funding for peace studies and sister fields disappeared or dwindled from coast to coast.

In many respects, though, the field of peace studies is itself partly responsible for the kind of ignorance exemplified by the notion that peace had arrived with the end of a war (cold or hot). For we have continued to study the absence of war and overt violence and call it "peace" for so long that we cannot expect many outside our conversations and essays to read the fine print. And even though there has been a fundamental shift in emphasis in most peace studies programs during the past decade away from so-called "negative peace" to so-called "positive peace," the damage done will take a long time to undo. Like metaphors, categories of thought can be extremely powerful and consequently can affect perception, analysis, and behavior far beyond the half-lives of diplomas. One of my hopes, therefore, is that we can move beyond the limitations and disadvantages of thinking in terms of positive and negative peace to devote our attention to *"essential peace"* (i.e., the essence of peace; what is essential if peace is to exist), rather than continue to be distracted by *"shadows of peace"* (i.e., not peace itself, but somber images of its absence) (Crews 1999).

Much of my work from 1987 to 1994, as founding executive director of the Peace Studies Association, involved working with others to enhance the field of peace studies on campuses throughout the United States (and on occasion, in Europe and South America). It was our collective task to both enhance and represent peace studies as a legitimate field of academic study to colleagues, faculty in general, department chairs, deans, chancellors, and presidents. What made this difficult, of course, were two critical factors: (1) the increasing competition for scarce resources on most campuses and (2) the discipline-based training and thinking of many in these otherwise diverse constituencies.

Those of us in peace studies, however, knew without a doubt that the field existed. With every course we taught, year after year, we immersed ourselves in the theories, critiques, methods, and solutions that defined the field. We came together at conferences and faculty development trips to discuss, critique, share, and learn from one another. We knew the field was comparatively young, but also knew it was solid, substantive, and enduring.

Initial Images of Service-Learning

Thus, I was quite surprised when I became involved in service-learning, attended my first conference in the fall of 1993, and discovered an entirely different community of actors and academicians who were directly or indirectly interested in issues of justice, conflict, and peace, but seemed to know little or nothing about the academic field of peace studies. I came away from that first conference with the sense that there was a staggering amount of discontinuity present within academia. But then, service-learning — its theories, methods, practitioners, and networks — was new to me too, so the lack of awareness was equally mine. Nonetheless, even using very conservative estimates, the field of peace studies was at least 45 years old at the time: The first undergraduate academic program in peace studies began at Manchester College in North Manchester, Indiana, in 1948. It seemed reasonable to me that teachers personally and professionally committed to peace and justice would have heard of peace studies.

This new community of teachers appeared to be academically situated in their disciplines and subject matter and primarily focused on pedagogy as a means of addressing justice and social change through higher education. Ironically, an entire field of study was available, waiting to be tapped. Peace studies is all about the analysis of social problems and conflict, theories of and strategies for social change, skills and techniques of empowerment and conflict resolution, and histories of successful nonviolent struggle (including education). Its substantive goals are identical to, or in close proximity to, some of the pedagogical goals of service-learning. This disjuncture between the service-learning and peace studies communities in academia prompted me to reflect upon my own ignorance of service-learning: What else did I need to know about its pedagogical benefits in order to be a more effective teacher in peace studies?

One of the confusions for me at the outset was that the motivations for employing service-learning among faculty at these conferences and work-shops seemed to vary considerably. Some faculty appeared to be interested in it because they taught courses that focused directly or indirectly on issues of justice, social responsibility, or leadership. Others seemed interested because they personally were concerned about issues of justice and wanted to find ways to integrate their concerns into their courses even though the subject matter they taught did not seem to warrant it. Faculty in a third group were not especially interested in issues of justice and peace, but saw service-learning as a viable pedagogy for enhancing learning, inculcating leadership skills and values, and increasing the participatory dimensions of education. And finally, a fourth group included those who appeared to be motivated solely by good will: They saw service-learning as a panacea for many problems beyond education, and wanted to transform it into a global "movement" (and here "movement" implies something quite different from Parker Palmer's advocacy of a "movement approach to educational reform" [1966]).

This wide array of motives and intellectual orientations toward service-learning kept me in a state of perpetual disequilibrium. In response to the first group, I found myself encouraging some modest immersion in peace studies: It seemed as though what they were already doing belonged within the fold, so embracing peace studies more directly made sense.

My reaction to the second group was one of concern: It seemed some were more interested in teaching students *their* values than in teaching *about* values. My own work in peace studies led me to advocate on behalf of teaching students to be critical thinkers and to question and examine their own values (and those of the societies in which they lived), instead of using the classroom as a moral bully pulpit. By this, I do not mean that education shouldn't involve the *whole* person (including ethical growth); rather, I mean that teaching the whole person precludes proselytizing and ideology cloning. Teaching the whole person demands that we respect one another, i.e., that we allow our students the same intellectual and moral freedoms we expect for ourselves.

Since I was involved in the subject matter as well as the pedagogy, I found I had little in common academically with members of the third group, who seemed to have minimal interest in the subject matter. Nonetheless, employing service-learning pedagogies solely for the purpose of enhancing learning seemed quite legitimate to me. After all, although it may not be reasonable to assume that all disciplines have questions of peace and justice as their central concern, all disciplines certainly should be free to reap the benefits of service-learning as pedagogy.

However, these various motivations for embracing service-learning raised other haunting questions for me: Was service-learning something more than a pedagogy? Was there academic subject matter involved? Could one major or minor in it, like English, biology, or peace studies? If so, what was the subject matter? If not, why were some (i.e., the fourth group of faculty) starting to embrace it as a social movement that would save us at all levels of society and transform our troubled world into paradise?

Reflections on Service-Learning and Peace Studies

First images are often poignant, but rarely are they sophisticated. Over the past few years, the people I have worked with in service-learning (both on and off campus) have continued to impress me with their pedagogical courage. As bell hooks has observed,

> . . . many teachers who do not have difficulty releasing old ideas, embracing new ways of thinking, may still be as resolutely attached to old ways of practicing teaching as their more conservative colleagues . . . it takes a fierce commitment, a will to struggle, to let our work as teachers reflect progressive pedagogies. (1994: 42-43)

As I reflected upon my colleagues in peace studies, I realized that some might benefit from the examples set by my colleagues in service-learning vis-à-vis pedagogical courage. I also noticed the latter's commitment to justice and their tenacious belief in the validity of their struggle, despite their awareness that they are innovators and "early adopters," i.e., despite the fact that the rest of society does not share their perspective, at least at present (and maybe for a long time to come). Thus, in many respects, faculty in service-learning resembled some of my colleagues in peace studies.

These similarities, however, extend to their mutual lack of familiarity with each other's efforts and pedagogies. This phenomenon has been most troubling and challenging for me, caught, as I have been, with one foot in peace studies and the other in service-learning. Of all the disciplines and fields of study, one would think that peace studies would be well-versed in service-learning. Today, some five years later, roughly the same situation persists: Finding enough contributors to fill this volume with essays on peace studies and service-learning was more difficult than either Kathleen Weigert or I ever imagined.

Humanizing Learning and Transforming Academia

As I mentioned at the outset, both peace studies and service-learning are "humanizing" agents in education. By this, I mean that they seek to (1) bring human beings back into the subject matter and the pursuit of knowledge and (2) personalize the learning process, i.e., allow students to participate more fully in their own education. What does this mean?

Over the years I have watched both undergraduate and graduate students react with increasing disappointment to the passive consumption of information and the cold impassiveness of the theories, analyses, textbooks, lectures, and labyrinthine bureaucratic rules, regulations, and requirements to which they have been subjected. They find themselves involved less and less in education-as-learning, entangled more and more in education-as-business. And the dominant mode of "learning" they are subjected to takes the form of what Paulo Freire calls "the banking concept of education" (1970: 58), or what Kalin Grigg, a service-learning colleague of mine in Durango, Colorado, more graphically refers to as "the bulimic model of learning."

What I have always valued most about peace studies is that it is about making the world a better place for everyone. It is education that is relevant to the world and to the personal lives of the students who pursue courses in it. Its subject matter, and sometimes its methods, connects the classroom with the "real" world off campus. Peace studies is an essential venue for gaining the courage and the skills needed to confront the troubles our world faces and to seek realistic solutions to them. Before it is too late. At its best, peace studies empowers students to learn about the world they inhabit, how others experience and see the world differently than they do, and how one can go about initiating constructive, nonviolent social change. Said differently, peace studies is not only about learning the value of caring about others but also about learning *how* to care about others, and doing so in ways that seek to transform the world, one's own life, and the lives of those in need.

What I value in service-learning is that, as pedagogy, it does exactly that: It connects the classroom and campus with the world students inhabit and the worlds they know nothing about. It offers them the opportunity to participate much more fully in their own learning. And, at its best, service-learning has the power to transform learning, perceptions, commitments, behavior, and, ultimately, our relationships with one another and the world. Not bad for a modest, unpretentious pedagogy. And, as if that weren't enough to persuade me, service-learning is a pedagogy that seeks to transform academia, too.

Although not all service-learning courses are successes, my guess is that it is increasingly difficult to find a teacher who has explored service-learning, integrated it into a class and then refined it over time, who will ever want to return to teaching the course the way she or he did before. Once teachers see how passionate and knowledgeable students become about what they are learning (because *they* are learning it), once they see how flexible and dynamic the pedagogy is in embracing nontraditional learning styles, and once they see how valuable the service is to both students and community partners and constituencies, they need little coaxing.

It has been my own experience as a teacher that service-learning gives the learning process a human face (for the students in my courses and for myself). This is not a claim that all teaching outside of service-learning fails in this regard: Many teachers and approaches do succeed in "putting a human face on learning." It is merely to acknowledge that to see and experience nonviolence at work through service, for example, is much more powerful than to read histories of it across distant decades and continents.

Pedagogies of Peace: Learning and Teaching as Social Change

Finally, as a way of constructing a small bridge between peace studies and service-learning that might carry at least a few colleagues from one side of the divide to the other, I want to invite a serious exploration of the pedagogies of peace.

Over the years I have consciously attempted to teach my peace studies courses in ways that do not contradict the subject matter. Especially in my Nonviolence courses (given how foreign nonviolent spaces are within our cultures of violence), it has been essential to establish a few simple ground rules at the outset: (1) we respect one another (we can agree and disagree freely with one another but must seek to respect one another); therefore (2) we must listen actively and carefully to what everyone in the class thinks and says (especially when we disagree); (3) we must seek to understand one another rather than trying immediately to find ways to disagree and "prove" others wrong and ourselves right; and, following from the above, (4) there is no interrupting.

One would think that such ground rules would not be necessary in adult environments in which freedom of thought and expression are guiding principles and that they would be easy to follow. I continue to be surprised at how difficult many students find them. They do so because the dominant modes of formal learning in academia have placed less value on listening to, understanding, and respecting others. What matters more is winning. And winning is achieved in academia by engaging in intellectual combat in the classroom and in the homework in order to show how "smart" one is to one's teacher and to others. Academic combat most often takes the form of debate, argumentation, and attack. One listens or reads or analyzes just long enough to discover a weak point in the other's "argument" and then critiques and attacks it (ideally before anyone else does). In this mode, "critical thinking" is misconstrued as "being critical of the other."

What has evolved in traditional pedagogies of this sort is an intellectual form of conducting violent conflict. We collectively condemn war and killing, but reserve the right to attack one another through our ideas and words in our classrooms and in our "academic" work. I do not use the word *violent* lightly here. According to Friesen (1986: 143), "The word 'violence' is rooted in the Latin verb 'to violate' which is the same in Latin as the verb 'to rape.' The word basically means to violate the dignity or integrity of a person." This kind of teaching and learning is violent because, at its core, it not only is disrespectful of (and does not care about) the other, it also violates the dignity or integrity of the other. As Gandhi learned so well during his lifetime, if we do not care about others' views, needs, and truths, we are not interested in collective truth; we are only interested in being the winner. In this "seek-out-weakness-in-the-other-and-then-attack" mode, we do not achieve a relationship with the other that could in any way be characterized as akin to what Martin Buber (1970) meant by "I and Thou" relationships.

This is not to imply that all debate and argumentation is inherently hostile, violent, or counterproductive. Clearly, even though much of it becomes arguing, some debate and argumentation can take place in ways that lead to collaborative, nonviolent learning. My own view is that the latter happens much less than the former. But what is becoming more and more evident and daunting to me is the extent to which we are not teaching peace, or justice, or social change. What we appear to be doing, through our more traditional teaching and learning styles, is advocating the values of win-lose competition dynamics over the pursuit of "truth" (with a very small, very personal "t"). What we are role-modeling in these pedagogies is not civil discourse but uncivil selfishness.

If this is in fact the case, what we have accomplished, while seeking to improve upon the status quo and enable constructive social change (in academia and the world outside our classrooms), is that we have, instead, become the status quo. And Pogo would have been right after all. As bell hooks puts it so well, it is " . . . the difference between education as the practice of freedom and education that merely strives to reinforce domination" (1994: 4).

Peace studies is certainly not the only legitimate subject matter to teach, and service-learning is not the only way to teach it. Service-learning is not a panacea for all of our problems, and we should not entertain unrealistic notions about teaching every class this way. What service-learning can do, however, is augment and enhance the positive aspects of traditional modes of teaching and learning in ways that will have profound effects upon academia and society. And if this is so, those of us in peace studies should be delighted to learn of its existence and its potential to assist us in the struggle to learn how to be a little kinder to others and ultimately make both academia and the world beyond it more peaceful and civil communities in which to reside.

References

Buber, Martin. (1970). *I and Thou.* Translated by Walter Kaufmann. New York, NY: Charles Scribner's Sons.

Crews, Robin. (1999). "Peace." In *The Oxford Companion to American Military History,* edited by John Whiteclay Chambers II. New York, NY: Oxford University Press.

Freire, Paulo. (1970). *Pedagogy of the Oppressed.* New York, NY: Seabury Press.

Friesen, Duane K. (1986). *Christian Peacemaking and International Conflict: A Realist Pacifist Perspective.* Scottdale, PA: Herald Press.

hooks, bell. (1994). *Teaching to Transgress: Education as the Practice of Freedom.* New York, NY: Routledge.

Palmer, Parker. (1966). "Divided No More: A Movement Approach to Educational Reform." *Higher Education Exchange:* 5-16.

Service-Learning as Education:
Learning From the Experience of Experience

by Michael Schratz and Rob Walker

What do students really learn in a service-learning program? Where are the gaps between service-learning as an espoused theory and as a theory-in-use? Does service-learning have a distinctive form of curriculum? What kinds of teaching and what student roles does service-learning require or encourage? What professional development do those teaching in service-learning programs need? How can service-learning best be assessed? What are the criteria for assessment? What evaluation and validation demands does service-learning face within higher education? What are the institutional pressures that stem from working in unconventional ways?

In this essay we cannot promise to answer all these questions, but we raise them at the outset to demonstrate that service-learning programs call for educational analysis and understanding. Just as service itself is not enough to secure student learning, so experience of the program is not in itself enough to justify it. For those involved in promoting and practicing service-learning within higher education programs, there is a need for reflection, analysis, and critical discussion of a range of educational issues.

Reflective Practice and Storytelling

In the way it is described in this monograph series, service-learning is clearly innovative, but also builds on a long-standing tradition of educational thought and practice. The educational assumptions that are made in service-learning programs relate service-learning to a family of educational ideas, at the heart of which lies the idea of learning by reflecting on experience. The idea that reflecting on experience is a key to human learning is probably almost as old as language itself. Being able to speak to ourselves and to others about what we experience provides a means of editing and rewriting the scripts of everyday life, provides the basis of a mental reference system for filing and storing significant memories, and allows us to build the narratives that give meaning and interest to our lives and those of others. Moreover, being able to replay life through talk provides the basis for much of what we find most engaging and compelling in human interaction.

Our experience of experiential learning in the related context of peace-building projects and of action research in the context of professional training suggests to us that, despite its immediate appeal, the standard definition of service-learning glosses significant educational issues. Between the community and the university, cooperation and common goals cannot be taken for granted: What one sees as "civic responsibility" another may see as "corruption." Between the competitive academic curriculum and learning from experience lie many traps for student and teacher. Once the curriculum steps outside the university, we have to be aware that we tread potentially dangerous ground among different social values, antagonistic cultures, and organizational practices.

Our intention in this essay is not to develop a critical attack on the notion of service-learning but to provide educational understanding of it. We do this in part to help defend the idea and the practice by attempting to close the gaps that inevitably grow between hope and happening.

The Ethnography of Learning

Central to service-learning is the belief that people learn from the experience of being placed in unfamiliar settings and expected to develop some degree of competency. In such circumstances the construction of narrative is a key learning process. We do not just "learn" in an abstracted way; we learn *from* someone, from doing things (particularly from our errors, misunderstandings, and mistakes), and from processing what we learn as stories. Such stories are not just peripheral, for the stories we tell our families and friends, at work and elsewhere, provide the basis on which we construct our sense of community and belonging. Learning, in this sense, is not simply the process of acquiring knowledge and skills, but because it involves language, it inevitably opens doors to multiple levels of discourse. It has both form and content, process and outcome; it is both social and cultural. As the anthropologist Jules Henry once wrote, education in humans is essentially *polyphasic* (1960: 268), which is to say we almost never learn only one thing at a time. The multidimensionality and reflexive potential of language lies at the heart of a culture's capacity to develop and to change. It follows that to place people in service-learning settings is not just to provide opportunities for them to learn, it is also to disrupt their lives.

As many Peace Corps workers discovered, to be placed in a service role in another culture is implicitly to be expected to act as an ethnographic researcher: learning about the culture by learning how to act as a useful member of it. As a theory of learning, this idea has been well developed by Jean Lave and her colleagues (Lave 1988; Lave and Wenger 1991). Through the cross-cultural study of activities as diverse as those performed by midwives, tailors, quartermasters, butchers, nondrinking alcoholics, and supermarket shoppers, they have developed a notion of apprenticeship as "legitimate peripheral participation." They see this as providing "a way to speak about the relations between newcomers and old-timers, and about activities, identities, artifacts and communities of knowledge and practice." Their aim is to understand how "a person's intentions to learn are engaged and the meaning of learning is configured through the process of becoming a full participant in a sociocultural practice," which, they argue, "subsumes the learning of knowledgeable skills" (Lave and Wenger 1991: 29).

The phrase "legitimate peripheral participation" seems to describe well the role of the service-learner as both inside and outside a workplace, community, or culture. Because of the context of their work, Lave and her colleagues see such a role as transitional, to be phased into full membership, but it can also be a role in which people get stuck. William Labov (1973), for instance, argues that marginality may be a terminal destination for outsiders who want to become insiders. Having studied the language of street gangs in Philadelphia and elsewhere, he argues that "lames," those kept at the margins, may appear to an outsider to be at the center, for they over-identify, amplifying those behaviors (dress, forms of speech, manner of acting) that to an outsider appear to be definitive. But taking this role inevitably places them in situations marked by transgression, for they find themselves being seen by those "inside" as anomalous: partly inside and partly outside, not clearly located by the boundaries and the relationships that define the roles of everyone else.

Placing people in a service role implies placing them not just in a new culture but to some degree at the margins of that culture. They are there to learn how to help a community bring about change, but they can only do this effectively by reflecting on the consequences of their actions, learning from mistakes, and making judgments about the motivations, commitments, and capabilities of those with whom they work.

There are parallels between the service role and the research role of the fieldworker, which, as anthropologists describe it, is a method that relates as much to identity as it does to technique. Paradoxically, to engage in effective action requires a fair degree of introspection. What we will learn most about when we try to change others is ourselves.

The Significance of Trivia

The "basic understandings" of social situations and cultures that ethnography provides are often built on a reassessment of the significance of trivia. What we first notice in any novel situation are the small things. When we travel, we retune our perceptions: We notice advertising, the way people dress, street signs, the items in shop windows, the graphic design of newspapers. Until we readjust our perceptions and return to a sense of "normality," it is as though our perceptions are amplified: We are aware that colors may seem brighter; we are able to recall, with some precision, particular scents and smells; we hear different sounds that the locals may not notice (the church bells from a distant village, the sound of a bamboo flute in the hills, the many sounds in a Harlem air shaft).

The same is true (though perhaps in a more mundane sense) of social and workplace situations and as our minds race to read social interaction, to search surface features in an attempt to detect power and influence, insecurity and resentment, pride and guilt, so these perceptions, too, can become amplified and distorted. And because we quickly become a part of these interactions, our perceptions of ourselves can be thrown out of their usual grooves. We notice what is trivial because we are forced to, for in a small way what we have to do is rebuild our lives. We have to learn, often very quickly, how to act appropriately. We do this by working back through our perceptions to a point where we can take things for granted, and the more alien the situation the further back we have to go.

So, one of the valuable, educational processes that service-learning encourages (perhaps surprisingly, given its aspirations) is regression to the trivial. Putting people into novel situations means they must retune their perceptions in order to rebuild their sense of self in the face of the expectations of a new social situation or new microculture. We all go through much the same process, to some degree or another, when we attend a new school, when a parent remarries, when we are sent to a school as a practice teacher, when our children are born, when we move, when we travel.

This is not just a comment on the social nature of perception, for there is a moral color to these observations of small things. In a new context, we usually find it hard to read the vital social signs, to know when we have acted inappropriately, transgressed, or misunderstood. Travellers may be tempted to romanticize small differences, but ethnographers and migrants inevitably experience the next stage in this process, which is a moral longing for the familiar (they miss all those things that were so much better back home). They become aware that there is a silence in their lives that was once filled with the small things from home: certain foods, flowers, music; the sound of a radio program; the customary ways in which people greet one another, laugh, celebrate, and grieve. Again, it is often the trivial things that loom largest, seemingly carrying an emotional traffic far outweighing their apparent significance. (A classic description of the homesickness felt by the ethnographer in the field can be found in Bronislaw Malinowski's diaries [1967]).

The word *trivial*, incidentally, was originally an educational word that has become diluted in contemporary everyday use. In medieval times it referred to the *tri via*, or three ways of knowing (logic, rhetoric, and grammar), which were seen to be at the heart of education. *Trivial* therefore meant not, as it does now, "things of little consequence" but knowledge that was so basic it could be taken for granted that an educated person would know it, what now might be called a "core curriculum," or perhaps a "liberal education."

So, if service-learning can reinstate the significance of trivia in the contemporary curriculum, this would be, in itself, a worthwhile aim. (A specific method for doing this — collaborative memory-work — we have described elsewhere [Schratz and Walker 1995].) Conventionally in academic discussions, to describe learning as "trivial" is to dismiss it, but if close attention to small things causes people to reassess and reevaluate the details of social life, the routine and day-to-day patterns of interaction, the variety of ways in which people interrelate in the workplace, then this provides a valuable counterpoint to the usual stuff of academic learning, which is often dominated by big ideas, large-scale concepts, and concerned mostly with explanation in the form of abstraction.

"Real" Learning

One of the features of service-learning is that it takes "learning" out of the academy in an attempt to make it "real." Although university learning has many distinctive, valuable, and hard-won features (its valuing of critical independence, its traditions of discussion and debate, its valuing of collaborative effort and disciplinary community), direct experience offers opportunities for the student to field-test what he or she has learned and to realize that institutional learning has inherent limitations. In an international study of the relationship between age groups and "learning projects" conducted in 1992-93, one of the authors asked people which learning experiences mattered to them as far as far-reaching consequences were concerned. All those interviewed (N = 30) agreed that school learning gave them a grounding on which to build, but none of them said that schooling was the most decisive factor in his or her learning career. On the contrary, many said that they could have used the time spent in school in more worthwhile experiences. Their feeling was that institutional learning was too far remote from what they actually experienced in real life to be of direct use.

In contrast to institutional learning, they often mentioned particular people who became important to them in their learning careers. It may have been a teacher in school who provided them with a role model or perhaps a distant relative or a friend. Some said they went into a job because of the influence of those significant others, or those others caused them to rethink their professional lives (especially when they felt they lacked self-assurance). Interestingly enough, significant others were rarely found within people's immediate families. Although fathers and mothers have an important influence on their children, they were not mentioned as decisive influences in these people's overall lives. Instead, most saw the family as a place they could always return to, where they could take time to step out from the routine of their lives.

They often mentioned their leisure time as offering opportunities for learning. Although some mentioned modern technologies, more often it was hobbies and sports that provided a challenge that had an educative influence. Moreover, the fields of learning people found significant were often very different from their professions, but indirectly the fields did have an impact on their work — either through networking (through hobby partners) or through skills that could be applied in their job situations.

In many people's lives there was a phase in which they got particularly interested in politics — either locally or nationally. Most interviewees commented that they involved themselves very little in politics while they were in school; however, they were more taken with politics when they suddenly felt like a *zoon politicon* (Greek for a "political being"). This "politicization" was in some cases like a process of personal awakening, but often this phase petered out again after some time; most people said they were rather frustrated about how politics worked — both on the micro and macro levels.

On the macro level, it was more often societal changes or challenges that had an influence on people's learning experiences. These were sometimes quite dramatic, as in the case of the fall of the Iron Curtain, which confronted people with completely new challenges in coping with a new reality. To a lesser extent, the influences were "movements" such as ecology or an influx of foreign people that made the interviewees aware of some kind of responsibility for global issues.

Finally, critical incidents had the deepest impact on the learning of these individuals. A critical incident is something that happens to one particular person and is often connected with loss. Loss of a partner, loss of good health, loss of work, and loss of freedom in the case of pregnant women were all examples of such incidents. They required more than just a readjustment to life; they possessed some transformational force related to rethinking central issues in people's lives.

The ideas just discussed, which build on Lave and Wenger's notion of "legitimate peripheral participation," and which relate both to adult education theory (for instance, Kolb 1984) and to experiential learning (Winter 1989), provide a link between the theory and practice of service-learning and the mainstream of educational thought. (See Figure 1 for a graphical depiction of the application of this approach to service-learning.)

A related distinction that is useful involves differences between "closed" and "open" learning: "Closed" learning signifies the traditional delivery of

Figure 1. Types of learning within service-learning

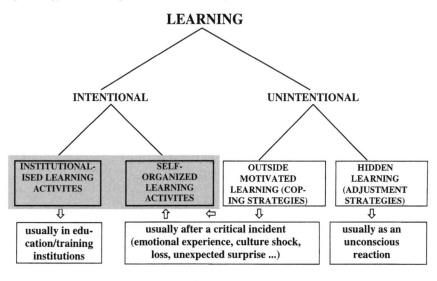

grey area covers the combination of institutionalised learning and
self-organised learning activities

Figure 2. Open and closed learning

	Closed Learning	Open Learning
Thinking Process	mechanistic	dynamic
Philosophy Behind	everything has to be fixed	living with insecurities
Point of Reference	central	local
Academic Strand	disciplinary	transdisciplinary
Orientation	curriculum-oriented	problem-oriented
Strategy	optimizing, maximizing	pervasive
Scheme	cause - effect	network
Teaching Structure	rigid	flexible
Type of Learning	knowledge-based	reflexive

knowledge; whereas service-learning is a form of "open" learning (see Figure 2 for an illustration of the differences between "closed" and "open" learning).

Service-Learning and the University

Our basic argument is that, content aside, the process of service-learning, by integrating experience, reflection on that experience, and communication about that experience, seeks to build on a social view of learning. Service-learning is not alone in this, but with action learning, action research, and other approaches it forms part of a spectrum of related ways of thinking about educational programs. What characterizes all of these forms of learning is that they are essentially cyclical and cumulative, and so quite different from the linear sequences of hierarchical objectives that characterize much academic learning and formal instruction. Rather than "theoretical analysis followed by practice," service-learning puts practice in the central position and then asks for reflection-on-practice: Its concern is not so much with having students acquire competence as with having them gain capability.

We have argued that the basic structure of the educational situations created by service-learning involves conceptual (and cultural) separations between the world of the academy — the university — and the "real world," each with its characteristic discourse, frames of reference, and habitus. Those academics engaged in service-learning as teachers find themselves moving to renegotiate and circumscribe their authority, not assuming that they know or understand all that their students are learning, but trying to place themselves in a role where they can stimulate, refocus, and sometimes rescue students as they set out on their own paths. This requires those students to move both ways, and to attempt to create a space within which they can talk about experience disconnected from the immediate need for action, and yet to do so with immediate implications for changes in action.

The Ethics of Exploration

When a student in a service-learning program is first situated in a workplace (which we take to include placement in an agency, community, or service site), there is initially a sense of incompetence that provides a starting point from which to learn. In one of our courses we explain this in terms of a developmental sequence that begins with recognizing the inability to cope. In the face of a crisis, learners need to move from

- *unconscious incompetence* (knowing we can't cope but not knowing why), to

- *conscious incompetence* (recognizing our failures), to
- *conscious competence* (finding ways to cope), to
- *unconscious competence* (coping without having to think how).

In this situation, the teacher appears to lose the power that derives from his or her role in the classroom. As the curriculum is seen to derive from students' experiences in placements, so the authority to define content appears to shift from teachers to students. Teachers therefore have to reconstrue their role at another level: Relevant knowledge now lies in process, in creating links between the reports students bring back from the field and knowledge that helps them frame these reports.

Recognizing that in conventional teaching the student culture is not just a mediating influence but a powerful element in the hidden curriculum, we have tried to turn this culture in on itself so that it becomes the very substance of the curriculum. But doing this is not just a question of teaching technique, for it exposes vulnerabilities in students (and perhaps in teachers) that are normally kept hidden.

A clear but complex ethical question comes to light in any teaching that involves playing with social situations that are beyond the reach of the teacher's capacity to control. Despite all the educational limitations of classroom teaching, the classroom does provide a space disconnected to some degree from "normal" life, within which the teacher can exercise a degree of authority to ensure fairness and a measure of protection for individuals who may be subject to prejudice, scapegoating, or distress. Once we release students into situations outside the classroom, they are inevitably thrown back on their own resources. When they manage this passage successfully, it is clear that it provides the basis for significant learning on several levels. But what of those who "fail"? Is their "failure" equally significant? Does it leave an impression on their lives that is stamped deeper than "normal" classroom failure? What of those who are driven deeper into a limited repertoire of coping strategies? And as teachers, what responsibilities do we have in such circumstances? Should we excise the notion of "failure" from our vocabulary of actions? Should we confront students on the grounds for their "success"? Should we aim to change students as people? What would it mean to try to work this way in the context of an educational bureaucracy with different aims in view?

Emphasizing the collaborative nature of service-learning provides a partial answer, but it remains partial as long as the culture of higher education places so much value on individual performance and success. Inevitably, most programs have to find for themselves points of compromise.

Service-learning requires a heightened level of commitment from all those involved. We, too, have to be prepared to cope with the tendency of idealism to transform itself into cynicism. Many students (and perhaps teachers too) who turn to peace studies courses do so out of a sense of idealism. They want to make the world a better place and find a role for themselves in which they can feel what they are doing is worthwhile. What some will find when they work inside organizations that are dedicated to peaceful purposes may surprise them! The emotional warfare, naked ambition, and exploitation found in some volunteer agencies dedicated to radical change may be unsurprising to those of us who have encountered it before, but it can precipitate culture shock when encountered for the first time. And when the experience is linked to an educational course, it is more difficult to walk away from because to do so invites an institutional judgment of failure.

If teaching involves placing students in circumstances that have the emotional volatility that we know is characteristic of many peace groups, environmental agencies, and action groups, then we have an educational duty to provide some escape routes as well as to develop ways of strengthening our students' survival capacities and moral resistance. This is not to argue for indoctrination, but to emphasize that we need to extend the boundaries of our teaching to do what we can to help students develop a strong sense of self-awareness. Placing people in disorienting circumstances as part of their course and then dealing only with conventional academic analysis back in school will be inadequate. We have to adopt ways of teaching that involve, and support, more of the person.

Finding ways of doing this within the university that are practical, convivial, and educationally justifiable, yet avoid becoming self-indulgent or exploitive, can mean treading a difficult line. As teachers, we have to be prepared to face criticism from colleagues and others who may see any move away from the lecture and seminar as ideologically dangerous or dabbling in New Age sentimentality. Yet we have to address the issues directly, for avoiding them may have the unintended outcome of cynicism or other counterproductive outcomes.

The Hidden Curriculum of Service-Learning

Some of the issues we have identified stem from service-learning's cross-disciplinary nature. Disciplinary organization is central to universities, and Tony Becher (1989) fittingly compares university disciplines to different tribal systems. They have their territories and boundaries, their fields of competition and their pecking orders within and between them, their tacit knowledge and hidden agenda, and their specific patterns of communication, publications, divisions of labor, hierarchies, and careers (Huber 1990: 24). As part of socialization into an academic discipline, everybody entering university life has to find a way into the scientific community by complying with its fundamental rules:

> *To function smoothly within the group of teachers, fellow students and sec-*
> *retaries, the student needs a considerable amount of know-how. Most of it*
> *will be acquired slowly through the interaction with others and without*
> *anyone ever making a deliberate effort to teach the newcomer the rules of*
> *the game. Nonetheless, failure to comply with these implicit rules will*
> *undoubtedly affect the student standing within the group. (Gerholm 1985,*
> *quoted in Becher 1989: 26)*

In contrast, the nongovernment agency or community organization in which the student is placed is unlikely to operate within a disciplinary framework, but more likely to be closely geared to an organizational goal, a set of immediate objectives, and a mission statement. Moving between these two sets of expectations can be difficult, especially since the underlying features of organizations are not often made explicit, or are so formalized as to be generally ignored in the day-to-day pressures of working life.

One of the areas in which there is likely to be different views is deciding what constitutes successful learning. The "good student" in one context may not be seen this way in another context, and what successful students may need to do is develop one face for the university and another at their placement site, for if they try to apply directly what they have learned in academia, they may be made to feel like "professional strangers" (Agar 1980). It is as if a chess player familiar with the conventional chessboard were to find that the rules no longer apply.

Service-learning values personal learning and also assumes there are no shortcuts to authentic learning from experience (i.e., experience must be the authority from which the learning derives). Academic learning does not make this assumption but does insist on the need for knowledge to be publicly accessible and available for criticism. Thus, service-learning can find itself poised between its recognition that learning from reflection on experience is essentially a personal process and its need (within the academy) to find ways of making this same learning publicly accessible and transparent. This is a critical issue but not one that has been extensively explored; Michael Eraut points out that "many of these important epistemological issues have only recently begun to attract widespread attention among those engaged in professional education" (1994: 14).

This general theme, however, has been the subject of long-running discussions in education. The late Lawrence Stenhouse, who was well-known for his curriculum development work, argues:

> *I take it that social science or social scholarship is a form of institution-*
> *alised co-operative endeavour to extend and deepen understanding. It deals*
> *in public knowledge, public critique, public techniques, and throughout*
> *them creates a tradition, accessible to people of reasonable ability and*

industry, within which contributions to knowledge and understanding can be made. By means of a collaborative public structure it enables fairly humdrum people to make contributions to human understanding of a kind which pre-scholarly societies received only from the outstanding visionary or sage. Social science is democratic in the sense that the community of social scientists shares knowledge in such a way that the work of the less able is strengthened by the work of the more able, and that critical principles are accessible in the light of which the most authoritative scholars can be called to account. (1993: 23-24)

Here Stenhouse makes a strong case for cooperative endeavors within scientific communities. If we see service-learning as a "co-operative endeavour to extend and deepen understanding," such an approach would seem to offer a bridge between the educational differences we have described. If research as a means of creating and testing new knowledge (the defining characteristic of academic work) can be defined as "systematic inquiry made public" (Stenhouse 1984: 77), then the move to "co-operative endeavours" pulls the practice of service-learning back into the ambit of academic analysis and critique.

Our response has been to try to turn issues such as this back into the curriculum itself. We would argue, for example, that it is not enough to provide curriculum activities that strengthen an individual student's repertoire of behaviors in dealing with emotional volatility in volunteer groups driven by political conviction. It is also important to develop a shared understanding as to why this is so and why conventional professional training rarely takes such issues seriously. Perhaps our sociological instincts and training drive us in this, but it seems that a university education must provide more than training. It must provide students with the intellectual capacities and resources to be able to reflect together on where they are and where they are going in terms of their educational progress. This means publicly questioning themselves, their teachers, and the institutions that form the social context of their lives. (To question is not necessarily to reject, even though rejection is a stage they are quite likely to encounter in this process.) As teachers, our role in supporting students in this process is not necessarily easy or comfortable; there will always be a sense of moral risk in what we do, but this is the question that, in itself, lies at the very heart of what peace studies means.

Peace and Peace Education

A neglected question for peace studies is what we mean by "peace" as a set of practices. Certainly in the European context, much of the conventional peace studies curriculum is defined in terms of its opposition to war or other forms of hostility, to the point that "peace" itself is in danger of disappearing into negativity. Even training in mediation and conflict resolution starts from the base assumption that we face situations of oppositional conflict. Peace is therefore almost defined as a null category, solely in terms of its opposition to violence.

Service-learning does have the potential to provide a different starting point, in that it leaves the definitions more open. Asking the question "What is peace?" in the context of direct experience of the workplace is always going to be difficult, complex, and worthwhile, if only because the answers are not easily realized. Peace studies needs understandings of peace that are less simplistic, less facile, less behavioral than those understandings that are in common use.

If we are to invoke concepts of violence as a way of defining "peace," then the concepts we need must cut deeper than the everyday, tabloid-press use of the term. We need a definition like Galtung's, who 25 years ago wrote: "Violence is here defined as the cause of the difference between the potential and the actual" (Galtung 1969). In curriculum terms, deferring closure on the meanings we ascribe to "peace" is a worthwhile, significant, and defensible aim, and one probably realizable through service-learning.

Environmental educators (following Lucas 1977) frequently distinguish among different approaches to environmental education curricula, distinguishing education that is "about" the environment from education "in" or "for" it. Education "about" is easily recognized, for it is what we mostly encounter in school and elsewhere. Education "about" peace can be found in many college courses, in textbooks and libraries.

Education "in" peace appears to be what most will encounter in service-learning programs. (In environmental education, education "in" the environment is most often found in camps and field trips and in outdoor education.) But ultimately what we aim to achieve is education *for* peace. We want to make a difference.

Education "for," whether our concern is with the environment, with peace issues, or elsewhere, can only be identified in retrospect, for significant educational effects are complex, unpredictable, and take time to emerge. Service-learning marks a significant step forward because it involves commitment, because it cannot be ethically neutral, and because it collapses the dysfunctional divide between objectivity and subjectivity. But whether service-learning is education *for* peace must remain unresolved in the short run.

References

Agar, M.H. (1980). *The Professional Stranger. An Informal Introduction to Ethnography.* New York, NY: Academic Press.

Becher, T. (1989). *Academic Tribes and Territories: Intellectual Enquiry and the Cultures of Disciplines.* Milton Keynes, UK: Open University Press.

Eraut, M. (1994). *Developing Professional Knowledge and Competence.* London: Falmer Press.

Galtung, J. (1969). "Violence, Peace and Peace Research." *Journal of Peace Research* 6(3): 167-191.

Henry, J. (1960). "A Cross Cultural Outline of Education." *Current Anthropology* 1(4).

Huber, L. (1990). "Disciplinary Cultures and Social Reproduction." *European Journal of Education* 25(3): 241-261.

Kolb, D.A. (1984). *Experiential Learning: Experience as the Source of Learning and Development.* Englewood Cliffs, NJ: Prentice-Hall.

Labov, W. (1973). "The Linguist as Lame." *Language in Society* 2: 81-115.

Lave, J. (1988). *Cognition in Practice: Mind, Mathematics and Culture in Everyday Life.* Cambridge, NY: Cambridge University Press.

————— , and E. Wenger. (1991). *Situated Learning: Legitimate Peripheral Participation.* Cambridge, NY: Cambridge University Press.

Lucas, A. (1977). "Disciplinarity and Environmental Education." In *Education and the Human Environment,* edited by R. Linke, pp. 179-192. Canberra: Curriculum Development Centre.

Malinowski, B. (1967). *A Diary in the Strict Sense of the Term.* Translated [from the Polish] by Norbert Guterman. London: Routledge & Kegan Paul.

Schratz, M., and R.Walker. (1995). *Research as Social Change.* London: Routledge.

Stenhouse, L. (1984). "Evaluating Curriculum Evaluation." In *The Problems and Ethics of Curriculum Evaluation,* edited by C. Adelman, pp. 77-86. London: Croom Helm.

————— . (1993). *A Perspective on Educational Case Study. A Collection of Papers by Lawrence Stenhouse,* edited by R.G. Burgess and J. Rudduck. Coventry: University of Warwick/CEDAR.

Winter, R. (1989). *Learning From Experience: Principles and Practice in Action Research.* London: Falmer Press.

Study, Act, Reflect, and Analyze:
Service-Learning and the Program on Justice and Peace at Georgetown University

by Sam Marullo, Mark Lance, and Henry Schwarz

The Program on Justice and Peace was born out of Georgetown University's self-identity as a Catholic and Jesuit institution, created to appeal to a national and international audience, with close proximity to the nation's Capitol and all who have a particular interest in national governance and international affairs. Georgetown University expects in its students and faculty an ecumenical acceptance of all people and creeds as equal and deserving of dignity.[1] We begin with this self-concept because it has played a crucial role in defining our program as a "justice and peace studies" program, rather than simply as a peace studies or peace and conflict resolution program. We believe that Georgetown's tradition and identity have played positive roles in the development of our program, its relatively easy acceptance by faculty and administrators, and its popularity among students.

We do not mean to suggest, however, that our self-identity provides a uniquely ideal rationale for integrating community service into a peace studies program. Rather, we wish to stress the importance of drawing upon the strengths of one's institutional identity in building a program. In our case, the rationale for integrating service-learning into the Program on Justice and Peace is derived from the university's emphasis on social justice, ethics, and service to others, as well as its programmatic commitment to international affairs.

In this essay, we outline the process through which we consciously created a peace studies program, including our decision to build in a service-learning requirement. We then discuss the program's requirements and our experiences with the introductory course, the senior seminar, and students' service-learning experiences (particularly the fourth credit option).

Integrating Jesuit Educational Philosophy, Service-Learning, and Peace Studies

The Georgetown University Program on Justice and Peace (PJP) began its operations in 1992-93. It is an undergraduate certificate program, comparable to a minor, requiring six courses and at least 40 hours of community service integrated into the program. The 40 hours of service can be integrated either by formally attaching a fourth credit option (a long-standing program that enables students to link cocurricular service with a course through a formal reflection process) to a PJP course or by doing the equivalent number of hours and integrating them into the program (via papers, journals, or some other form of reflection) without receiving an additional credit. The program has experienced significant growth and increased support across the campus over the last five years, from granting one certificate in its first year of operation to 20 in 1995-96. There were 42 students enrolled in the program for 1996-97. This tremendous increase in numbers has forced us to restrict our course enrollments, to allow priority for certificate students to enroll in PJP classes, and to tighten admissions criteria for entry into the program. We believe that we have tapped a latent demand among our students, creating a program that enables them to act on their best intentions to be a force for positive change in the world. To facilitate this creativity, our definition of the community service work that can be integrated into the program is quite broad, enabling students to work at the local community level, the national program or policy level, or at the international level.

The Jesuit educational philosophy emphasizes intellectual rigor, critical inquiry, imaginative capacity, and service to others. Through a series of university-wide self-studies, the faculty have some widely shared ideas about the distinctive characteristics of a Jesuit education. Broadly defined, the educational goals of the university include a special recognition of the role of service in developing in students "intellectual and moral qualities that enable them to become competent, visionary, and wise persons who will lead flourishing lives while being ethically responsible and committed to serve with compassion the diverse communities within which they live and work" (CALLS 1995).

In addition to service, a strong commitment to social justice permeates the Jesuit program. The documents of the 34th General Congregation of the Society of Jesus make clear that providing service is only one of three essential components of promoting social justice: " . . . every Jesuit ministry can and should promote justice in one or more of the following ways: (a) direct service and accompaniment of the poor; (b) developing awareness of the demands of justice and the social responsibility to achieve it; and (c) participating in social mobilization for the creation of a more just social order" (General Congregation 1995). At Georgetown, this social justice commitment is demonstrated in the school's substantial ethics requirement, active extracurricular community service activities supported by the Volunteer and Public Service Center, medical and legal education that requires community-based clinical experience, and numerous other programs.[2]

The pedagogy that we envision linking social justice education with action and service is a four-step social analysis model: study, act, reflect, and analyze. These steps are conceptualized as a circular or spiral process, with action and reflection continually leading to deeper understanding, further study, and then more action and reflection. This pedagogy is well-suited for students to improve their understanding of the underlying causes of social problems, violence, and injustice. Their actions to ameliorate these problems expand their understanding of the complex structural, cultural, and human dimensions of oppression, discrimination, disenfranchisement, conflict, and deprivation. Whether students do service work in the area of human rights or homelessness, arms control or domestic violence, their work is enhanced by their class readings, lectures, and discussions, while their inspiration to learn more is motivated by the challenges that they confront in their work.

We stress that our emphasis on the connections between Georgetown's Jesuit and Catholic heritage and both the Program on Justice and Peace and service-learning should not be taken to suggest that a single perspective is universal among our faculty and students, much less institutionally required. To the contrary, our program brings a wide range of approaches — theoretical, methodological, and practical — to the study of these issues. We see the Jesuit and Catholic heritage of the university as a resource to be drawn on in creating an open intellectual dialogue and as one important voice taking place within that dialogue. But our program as such does not have any commitment to any particular ideology and welcomes active debate of all issues.

Linking Peace With Social Justice

We began our program with five faculty members meeting to create a peace studies initiative. Of the five, only one had formal graduate training in peace and conflict resolution studies, although three of the other four were committed to and experienced with peace issues in one form or another. This discussion process turned into a two-year study group, as we educated ourselves about the field of peace studies.[3] Throughout the process, we asked ourselves how peace studies should be incorporated into the curriculum, how such a program would be distinctive, and how we could take advantage of faculty expertise. It soon became clear that although we started out to create a peace studies program, our emphasis would lie in linking peace with social justice. Our reasons for doing so were conceptual, empirical, normative, and pragmatic.

On a conceptual level, it is our belief — following Galtung (1969) — that an image of positive peace cannot be present without the social structures that lead to justice. From an empirical point of view, one cannot study either of these phenomena in isolation. Structures of social oppression, actual or perceived, are among the major causes of war and other kinds of violent conflict. Such conflict also has obvious consequences for the social conditions necessary for justice. On the normative level, one cannot evaluate the ethical implications of violence without considering the consequences it has for social and political structure, and conversely, any adequate understanding of the fundamental political virtue of justice must at least outline the conditions under which people ought to be free from violence and war. Pragmatically, our interest was to create a peace studies program that differed from the arms control and diplomacy courses offered in the School of Foreign Service, placing a greater emphasis on positive peace and social justice, in contrast to the Foreign Service School's focus on negative peace (avoidance of war) and *realpolitik*. Our pragmatic interests also led us to include a service-learning requirement — we believe that the most effective way to learn about social justice is to practice it as well as study it.

Justice and Peace Studies Requirements at Georgetown

The PJP is a certificate program that requires six courses. Students begin their work in the program by taking Introduction to Justice and Peace, a course that presents a wide range of theoretical perspectives on social justice, poverty, hunger, racism, sexism, violence, and oppression. Students then select four electives in consultation with a faculty adviser, a combination that enables them to concentrate on particular problems and aspects of the field. Finally, students take a senior seminar in which they write a major paper on some aspect of peace and justice. These papers can involve empirical research, normative reflection, programmatic action plans, or conceptual analyses. They are produced under the guidance of a faculty mentor expert in the particular topic, as well as the professor in the seminar. In any one of these six courses, students may take a fourth credit option; otherwise, they may fulfill their service-learning requirement by enrolling in a course that has community service integrated into it.[4]

In the first two years of the program, the courses were drawn almost entirely from existing departmental course offerings, since we had virtually no budget. In the case of the introductory course, the idea was to supplement a core course on philosophical ethics (taught by one of the program directors) with frequent lectures by the other director, a sociologist, as well as with occasional guest lectures by others. The result was a mixed success. Required ethics courses at Georgetown all have between 65 and 70 students, some of whom are far from enthusiastic about their work. Thus, the sort of focused, exciting environment one wants in introducing students to a field was lacking.

Despite such practical difficulties, the program was surprisingly popular with both students and faculty. We quickly formed an energetic faculty committee to administer the program, with participants from numerous departments and the Dean's Office of each undergraduate school. Student interest also grew quickly, and to our surprise was strongest in the School of Foreign Service (SFS). This student enthusiasm was crucial to overcoming ideological opposition to approving PJP as a certificate program in the SFS. The majority of the work pushing the program through an initially reluctant governing committee was done by our first graduate and an assistant dean in the School. After being approved as a certificate program in SFS, enrollment in PJP grew by a factor of three in each of the next three years.

A major change in our program emerged in 1996-97. At the end of 1995-96, faced with enormous student growth, the curricular difficulties mentioned above, and increasing demands on faculty time, we went to the dean of Georgetown College with a request for increased funding. Essentially, we felt that without a greater institutional commitment to the program, we would be unable to accommodate increasing student demand. The result of that meeting was an increase in our budget to around $18,000. Though still small by comparison with the budgets of traditional departments, this sum has allowed us to offer an introductory justice and peace course and a senior seminar devoted exclusively to the program. In addition, we can now give a course release to a director, freeing up valuable time for administration and outreach.

Service-Learning: The Fourth Credit Option

In order to add a fourth credit option to a course, students write a service-learning contract at the beginning of the semester, indicating what service they will do, where the service will take place, and how the service work will be reflected upon or analyzed in conjunction with the course. Pending faculty approval, students undertake their service work and either write a paper, keep a journal, make presentations to the class, or carry out some other sort of analysis and reflection on their work.

The type of work that students can do and the sites at which they can serve are defined broadly, but must meet the following criteria: (a) they may provide direct services to individuals, groups, or a community (local, national, and/or global) that can be considered to be in need, oppressed, marginalized, discriminated against, underrepresented, handicapped, or otherwise disadvantaged; (b) they may provide support for challenging and/or changing existing social structures to the ultimate benefit of such a group in need; (c) they may engage in research that will contribute to policy discussions and/or change on pressing social problems; or (d) they may provide technical support to carry out policy discussions on pressing social problems. The course professor is responsible for evaluating the additional student work that demonstrates the link between the community service and the course's contents.

Students have completed fourth credit options in the introductory and elective courses by serving with a wide range of peace and justice organizations, including Women Strike for Peace, the Catholic Worker, the Ethics and Public Policy Center, Lorton Prison, the Coalition for the Homeless, Calvary Women's Shelter, and Amnesty International.

We are fortunate to have a Volunteer and Public Service Center in the Office of Student Affairs to support student voluntary community service and student service organizations. The center also supports the fourth credit option program by providing information and assistance to students with regard to locating service sites; transportation, training, and other logistical needs; serving as a central clearinghouse for doing the administrative work related to service-learning contracts and registration changes; and organizing midsemester and end-of-semester evaluation, writing, and reflection sessions for students.

Conclusions: Continuing Issues – Funding, Staffing, and Legitimacy

We are fortunate to be able to build a justice and peace studies program in a context that is supportive of service-learning. As noted above, the university has an ideological commitment to service firmly embedded in its mission, as well as an infrastructure in place to facilitate student involvement in community service. We were deliberate in emphasizing these commitments in the development of our Program on Justice and Peace, an emphasis that has paid off in terms of student and faculty support. This is not to say that there are no challenges confronting the program. The two major difficulties we face stem from limited resources and continued questioning of the program's academic legitimacy. We close our discussion with a brief summary of how we are addressing these challenges.

In a time of severely limited university budgets, new programs have to compete with existing programs and departments for a redistribution of resources, or generate new revenues for themselves. In terms of staffing, we have been fortunate to recruit top-notch faculty and encourage them to modify their courses to better fit the needs of the program. We have also been able to take advantage of in-place resources, such as lecture funds and faculty development resources, to bring speakers to the campus and to develop new courses. Our next step is to find external funding, through grants and targeted fundraising, to endow the program.

The second challenge we face is the continued questioning by a few faculty members of the legitimacy of peace studies and service-learning. Although we feel we have demonstrated the academic rigor of the program by adopting standards comparable to other interdisciplinary programs, and by stressing the academic, analytical component of service-learning, there continue to be skeptical questions and "backlash" reactions directed at the program. We have been, and continue to be, direct in addressing the concerns raised by skeptical colleagues whenever they occur. By keeping our deans well-informed, by educating our departmental colleagues, and by gaining the support of appropriate academic councils and curriculum committees, we have been able to avoid any serious threats to the legitimacy of the program. We have also been fortunate to recruit some top-quality students into the program. The success of our early cohorts of graduates and the high visibility of PJP-sponsored activities on campus have further solidified the program's reputation.

By carefully crafting our Program on Justice and Peace to fit the university's mission and by drawing on its commitment to service, we have effectively made service-learning a required component of the justice and peace certificate. By attending to the political and economic constraints and challenges of our environment, we have avoided the pitfalls that could have hampered our growth and have gained allies among key actors at the university. Although we have a great many challenges before us, the outlook for the continued development of justice and peace studies and service-learning at Georgetown University is comparatively bright.

Notes

1. This description is paraphrased from the *Georgetown University Bulletin*, which summarizes the university's mission statement.

2. This names but a few of the university's major social justice and community service initiatives. An audit of 1994-95 community service initiatives conducted by the Office of Planning and Institutional Research estimated that the university contributed more than 220,000 hours of community service and had paid direct costs of more than $4 million in operating community service programs.

3. A number of sources that we found to be particularly helpful in developing our program were Lopez (1989), Stephenson (1989), Mulch (1989), Kriesberg (1991), Benedict (1989), Bryan (1989), National Conference of Catholic Bishops (1983), and the syllabi collection in Thomas and Klare (1989).

4. The university offers several community service seminars built on service-learning principles. PJP students may enroll in these courses as electives and serve at an appropriate site to fulfill their service-learning requirement.

References

Benedict, Kennette. (July 1989). "Funding Peace Studies: A Perspective From the Foundation World." *The Annals of the American Academy of Political and Social Science* 504: 90-97.

Bryan, Dale. (1989). "Internship Education in Peace and Justice Studies: The Tufts University Experience." In *Peace and World Order Studies: A Curriculum Guide,* edited by D. Thomas and M. Klare, pp. 95-101. Boulder, CO: Westview Press.

CALLS. (1995). "Georgetown University Community-Action-Learning-Leadership-Service." President's Task Force on Community Service, Georgetown University.

Galtung, Johan. (1969). "Violence, Peace, and Peace Research." *Journal of Peace Research* 6: 167-191.

General Congregation. (April 1995). "Documents of General Congregation 34." *National Jesuit News:* 1-38.

Kriesberg, Louis. (1991). "Conflict Resolution Applications to Peace Studies." *Peace and Change* 16(4): 400-417.

Lopez, George. (1989). "Conceptual Models for Peace Studies Programs." In *Peace and World Order Studies: A Curriculum Guide,* edited by D. Thomas and M. Klare, pp. 73-86. Boulder, CO: Westview Press.

Mulch, Barbara. (July 1989). "Institutionalizing Peace Studies in College Life." *The Annals of the American Academy of Political and Social Science* 504: 80-89.

National Conference of Catholic Bishops. (1983). *The Challenge of Peace: God's Promise and Our Response. A Pastoral Letter on War and Peace, May 3, 1983.* Washington, DC: United States Catholic Conference.

Stephenson, Carolyn. (1989). "The Evolution of Peace Studies." In *Peace and World Order Studies: A Curriculum Guide,* edited by D. Thomas and M. Klare, pp. 9-19. Boulder, CO: Westview Press.

Thomas, Daniel, and Michael Klare, eds. (1989). *Peace and World Order Studies: A Curriculum Guide.* 5th ed. Boulder, CO: Westview Press.

Justice and Peace Studies at the University of St. Thomas

by David Whitten Smith and Michael Haasl

The University of St. Thomas (Minnesota) began planning its Justice and Peace Studies program in 1985, in response to the U.S. Catholic bishops' pastoral letter *The Challenge of Peace: God's Promise and Our Response* (National Conference of Catholic Bishops 1983). Members of the interdisciplinary planning committee urged that the program have a strong spiritual component. The founding and current director, David Smith, is a member of the Department of Theology. The program and minor were launched in 1987; the major was approved in December 1991. Five to 10 majors graduate from the program each year.

The Justice and Peace Studies program is designed to teach students how to criticize societies responsibly and to act effectively for the common good, both to relieve suffering and to make positive changes in social structures. Through interdisciplinary and experiential study, the program proposes a new way of looking at the world and responding to it. For justice and peace studies to be effective, concurrent experience with individuals on the margins is crucial. Life on the margins invites one to see and feel the world through the eyes of more vulnerable populations and to ask radically new questions, or old questions with radically new insight and passion. New questions lead to new analysis, to new understanding and judgment, and to new possibilities for appropriate action. Such experiential learning is no less a "revolutionary praxis" for mainstream, middle-class North Americans than Paulo Freire's (1970, 1973) liberating pedagogy is for poor Latin Americans and other oppressed peoples. Both forms of learning change worldviews, broaden narrow frameworks, put people into a dialogue with history, and empower them to be subjects of their own history.

Structure of the Program

The Justice and Peace Studies minor requires two core courses and three electives chosen from a list of appropriate courses, for a total of 20 semester hours. The major requires five core courses and five electives, some of which include "insertion" experiences (i.e., being with those who suffer injustice or poverty), and an internship. Students are also required to engage in additional "insertion" experiences through self-chosen service activities that are listed explicitly in their program. They are continually challenged, through class discussion and major-field advising, to relate these experiences to their coursework. The five core courses (the first two shared with the minor) are described in the sections below, followed by a brief outline of the "circle of praxis," upon which both the structure of the program as a whole and the structure of certain individual courses, especially the introductory and capstone courses, are based.

Core Courses

Introduction to Justice and Peace Studies (JPST 250) discusses what the world is like and how it operates, explores what a better world might look like, and considers the ways people try to move toward such a "better world." Each student studies a country through a series of steps that include vicarious experience, a consideration of human rights and the distribution of resources and power realities, a media study, possible actions, and a personal action step. In Theologies of Justice, Peace, Prosperity, and Security (THEO 305), students seek to view the world through someone else's eyes. Each student studies a religion or worldview different from his or her own through a series of steps similar to those in Introduction to Justice and Peace Studies. Active Nonviolence (JPST 450), taught by an experienced activist, allows students to learn vicariously the teacher's experience of active nonviolence in support of social change.

Conflict Resolution (JPST 470) emphasizes how groups form, grow, struggle, and mature or die. The learning experience is structured so that the class itself lives through these processes during the course of the semester. Different people have different preferred styles for working with conflict, as well as different basic personality styles (Myers-Briggs). The teacher explains these differences as God-given gifts, all of which need to be present in a healthy society. The final core course, Methods and Resources (JPST 472), returns to the Twin Cities, especially poor inner-city neighborhoods. It applies peace studies research to local communities, especially through the students' internships and other relevant activities. With the help of a service-learning coordinator, each student selects these at the beginning of the course to focus the semester's study. This course also teaches how to read and use statistics validly and responsibly and how to spot manipulation. Statistics that relate to the students' internships and service activities are drawn upon.

Service-Learning and the Circle of Praxis

The program uses a four-stage process — the circle of praxis: (1) a personal or vicarious ("insertion") experience of violence, poverty, and injustice; (2) a descriptive analysis of the economic, political, and social realities of a culture — how it operates (structures of distribution, decision making, and power) and the historical events that produced those realities; (3) a normative analysis that challenges existing societies on moral grounds, studies alternate possibilities (including radically new structures), and analyzes the moral values at stake; and (4) selection of action possibilities — identifying policies, strategies, skills, and actions needed to transform society from its present condition to a better condition; experimenting with these; and reexperiencing the transformed situation from the standpoint of the disadvantaged.

Introduction to Justice and Peace Studies and Methods and Resources explicitly introduce and integrate all four of these stages. Other courses emphasize one or more stages, while connecting them to the others. For example, Active Nonviolence and Conflict Resolution concentrate on action possibilities (stage 4), and the former relates these to Noam Chomsky's descriptive and normative analysis of current societies (Chomsky 1988, 1993; Herman and Chomsky 1988). Theologies of Justice, Peace, Prosperity, and Security concentrates on normative analysis (stage 3). Elective courses in the social sciences normally concentrate on descriptive analysis (stage 2), while those in theology and philosophy, such as Christian Faith and the Management of Wealth, concentrate on normative analysis (stage 3). The required internship concentrates on insertion (stage 1) and action possibilities (stage 4).

Stage One: Experience of Poverty and Injustice: Educational and leadership elites often study problems such as poverty without seriously consulting poor people. In such an atmosphere, theory can develop without much control by reality. This is not the way we want students to study the world, and we have many resources for "inserting" students into the experience of poverty and injustice. As an urban university, St. Thomas can place students in service opportunities and internships in many poor and disadvantaged communities suffering violence and injustice. Campus Ministry directs service programs locally, nationally, and internationally, and the university places a large number of students as tutors to disadvantaged grade school, high school, and alternative school students. Many majors find their own experiences and internships. The Justice and Peace Studies program, especially the Methods and Resources course, helps them reflect on what they are learning from these experiences.

The program also strongly encourages interuniversity programs and study abroad. The Higher Educational Consortium for Urban Affairs sponsors semester-long service-learning programs in Scandinavia, Colombia/Ecuador, and Minneapolis-St. Paul. The Center for Global Education, at Augsburg College, sponsors Latin American study semesters that emphasize service-learning.

When students first come to discuss a major, they begin by filling out a form that will follow them through their university careers; it lists their courses and activities (including extracurricular service) and shows how these relate to each other. Thus, students are encouraged from the beginning and at each semester as they register to think about all four of the stages of the circle of praxis.

Experiences with marginalized people have to be processed carefully lest the students notice only what reinforces their stereotypes. Introduction to Justice and Peace Studies requires an "urban dip" (small "urban plunge"). The typical urban plunge drops students into the middle of a poor urban neighborhood with only a few dollars in their pockets and challenges them to meet their basic needs for several days without the aid of their accustomed resources. An urban dip puts them into interaction for at least a few hours with poor urban residents in their own environment. Students are asked to write out their expectations before all experiences and to respond to a series of questions afterward that connect the experience to key concepts of the course. For example, students who tutor are asked: Do you see any signs that your students are experiencing discrimination in or outside of school? What attitudes do they have toward the local police and the school authorities? What has caused the school and neighborhood conditions your students live in? What realistic hopes might one have for a better situation in your school and its neighborhood? What actions might move from the present situation toward that realistic better situation? (See "Questions for Students Who Tutor as Part of the 'Urban Dip'" at the end of this essay.)

Students who tutor for extra credit in Theologies of Justice, Peace, Prosperity, and Security process their experience through questions such as the following: (1) How do your tutees' worldviews differ from your own — for example, regarding the purpose of human life? What more might you need to do to step into your tutees' experiences? (2) How would you apply the three "power questions" (Who is making the decisions here? Who is benefiting from the decisions? Who is paying the cost?) to your tutees? (3) How well has the principle of "subsidiarity" been applied in your school and your tutoring job?

One student reflected on her experience in the drop-in center Peace House:

> From appearances, the average person would judge Pat and Priscilla and Angel and Richard as not having a whole lot to give. But the stories they had, the experiences they'd been through and learned from, the rough times they had only taught them valuable lessons . . . those people were rich with knowledge about surviving and adapting and sharing and loving that no amount of money can ever get the "average person." I am fully aware that I didn't do a thing for the people who drank coffee at Peace House that day

— they were the ones who showed me a thing or two about living a quality life and valuing friends above all else.

Students receive extra credit in Introduction to Justice and Peace Studies when they choose to fulfill their urban dip experience through an alternative spring break week-long service project in such places as Appalachia; St. Vincent, West Indies; and the Turtle Mountain Indian reservation. (Students can also combine an alternative spring break or a similar month-long January term experience with individual study for course credit.) One student reflected as follows on her experience on an Indian reservation:

> *I went in expecting to see people in poverty with little hope. The thing that struck me the most about Turtle Mountain reservation is the positive attitudes that were present.*
>
> *Although there are problems on the reservation, they look towards bettering things instead of dwelling on the things that are not good. . . . It is inevitable that alcoholism will touch each person on the reservation in some way, through the family, friends, or a person themselves. To try to combat such a problem, alcohol awareness is prominent. The problems are admitted, now it is a matter of doing something to fight the problems. I have to say that I admire that very much.*

In the capstone course (Methods and Resources), students are introduced to poor and oppressed people who are responding energetically to their situations. They study how structural barriers prevent these people from being as successful as their abilities should allow, and the students are invited to *cooperate* with the poor who are working to transform unjust structures, rather than just to *serve* them as if they were helpless. Some poor people are disadvantaged as a result of disease, injury, or lack of education and experience. In such cases, students ask whether structural factors have led to these conditions. This topic of structural barriers moves them on to the second stage.

Stage Two: Descriptive Analysis: Core courses teach students how to understand structures of power and control that pattern human life. In addition, majors choose at least one other course in descriptive analysis, typically in the social sciences or history. Service-learning provides students with experiences of societal phenomena that social sciences set out to explain. Students are encouraged to explore questions such as: Why does such poverty exist? If people work 14 hours a day, why can't they put enough food on the table to eat? If enough resources exist and people are willing and able to work, why can't we organize our society to meet everyone's basic needs? Is there some larger flaw in our systems that defeats our efforts to organize work?

Methods and Resources relates students' internships and service to theoretical writings on peace studies. Discussions apply Johan Galtung's distinctions among "center," "periphery," "center of the periphery," and marginalized "periphery of the periphery" to local issues (1989: 22-27). One year the course examined a particular neighborhood in Minneapolis; another year it explored "center" and "periphery" in a nuclear energy dispute, when Northern States Power wanted to build nuclear waste storage drums at the edge of the Prairie Island Dakota reservation. Who in the power company might be "periphery of the center" — a possible ally? Who on the reservation might be "center of the periphery"? What groups and individuals hold power and how do they exercise it? Who benefits from the decisions made and who pays the costs? Justice and peace studies goes beyond "the way things are" to challenge and critique current structures and propose better alternatives. This leads to stage 3.

Stage Three: Make a Normative Analysis: Normative analysis (1) judges the current situation and (2) imagines a better one. Unless one can imagine a better situation, one won't challenge injustice and violence in the current system. Majors engage in normative analysis in their core courses and in one additional course of their choice. To judge the current situation, one needs an accurate picture of it — not just theories, but the reality experienced in stage 1. Indeed, we believe our students need to feel anger by sharing the frustration of marginalized peoples.

In Introduction to Justice and Peace Studies and in Theologies of Justice, Peace, Prosperity, and Security, students study countries, experiences, worldviews, and values very different from their own and relate them to justice and peace. Casting their net beyond the United States, before the modern period and outside the middle class, students can better imagine alternative possibilities. When they return to their own traditions, their experience on the margins may lead them to interpret those traditions in new ways and to reconsider the norms they use to make judgments.

Introduction to Justice and Peace Studies and Theologies of Justice, Peace, Prosperity, and Security ask students to write a utopia. Utopias help people break out of the ordinary, recognize the damage caused by structures normally taken for granted, and see new possibilities. Then students are asked to explain the barriers preventing their utopia from being realized and to propose a "possitopia," which is an improvement on present reality and is realistically achievable, but only if appropriate actions are taken.

Johan Galtung (1989: 28-32) encourages two forms of "self-reliance" in which a local community practices a sort of "import substitution" in order to keep the intellectual challenge of planning and entrepreneurship within the community. In Methods and Resources the class visits models of such self-reliance in the Phillips neighborhood: a housing service that provides mortgages that banks refuse to provide and a "reuse center" that markets used building materials and fixtures and provides expert advice and self-help training to local homeowners.

In Active Nonviolence, students are asked, What are your deepest private thoughts, feelings, and spiritual yearnings? Your task in life is to live those out in a commensurate way in public. The instructor then adds:

> *If you come into the justice and peace movement, you will come in at your own pace, with your own style and insights. These are mine, these are Howard Zinn's, these are David Dellinger's, Vernon Bellecourt's . . . people who live what they feel and believe. Before this class you did not know this history. Now that you know, you have a problem: What are you going to do about it? How will you live?*

This final question moves students to stage 4.

Stage Four: Making and Carrying Out an Action Plan: Unless one seriously asks who can do what, when, where, and how to move society toward justice and peace, analysis will remain "merely academic" in the pejorative sense. Hence, the student is invited to ask: Now that I understand the world in a radically new way, what am I going to do, if I am to remain authentic?

In addition to the urban dip, Introduction to Justice and Peace Studies asks students to do something constructive for the country they are studying. One student wrote to a prisoner in Northern Ireland (and later visited him in prison); another wrote President Bush urging him to relieve Brazil's debt burden; one taught a grade school class about Jamaica and had the children write to schoolchildren there; another wrote a powerful poem about Ireland; another composed and professionally recorded a song "Evil Find a Home Far Away From Here"; one chose to eat less animal protein; and another gathered clothing to donate to the poor.

In Active Nonviolence, the current instructor gives students the option of participating in his campaigns. Currently he is challenging Alliant Tech Systems, the largest producer of land mines in the United States, "to convert to peaceful production with no loss of jobs." Students write reflection papers connecting class readings, discussions, experience outside class, and their own life experience.

This course raises the question of what should count as "service." Do we implicitly identify service with relief work — doing things for people that they are too poor, inexperienced, or overwhelmed to do for themselves? Is it service to help people design and implement alternative structures to meet their needs outside dominant structures? Is it service to agitate for structural changes to remove unjust barriers that keep people unnecessarily poor? Is it service to challenge an oppressive "social peace" so that its hidden violence becomes exposed? The instructor claims that a life of resistance to unjust power is a life of service for the people and tends to attract students who are already doing service-as-relief work. Using Noam Chomsky's analysis, he challenges them to experiment with service that takes the form of advocacy or social change and helps them process their experiences (Chomsky 1988, 1993; Herman and Chomsky 1988).

In short, service-learning is implicated in all four stages of the circle of praxis, although one stage may receive more attention in a particular case. Justice and peace studies service-learning puts students into personal interaction with poor and oppressed people (stage 1: "insertion") and gives them experience in planning and carrying out actions to meet social needs (stage 4: "action plan"). As students reflect in class on their service, they draw upon political, economic, psychological, and social analyses of the dynamics that underlie the poverty and injustice they are experiencing as well as the history that led to the present situation (stage 2: "descriptive analysis"). They also engage in moral analysis to judge the current situation in the light of alternative world visions as they debate and experiment with various alternative structures and options for change (stage 3: "normative analysis"). At whatever stage of the circle students are engaged, they are challenged to relate that stage to the other three, testing theory against experience and seeking insight for new possibilities through theory.

Conclusion

The Justice and Peace Studies program at the University of St. Thomas can be characterized by the motto of Pope Paul VI, "If you want peace, work for justice," and by Pope John Paul II's call for solidarity with the poor and oppressed. Solidarity, fostered by the experience inherent in service-learning, clarifies our vision, builds our compassion and sense of community with the poor, and gives us the courage to work for justice and peace. The circle of praxis, experienced through service-learning, provides a framework and practical guidance. With these skills and insights, graduates of our program have done us proud. We trust they will continue to do so.

References

Chomsky, Noam. (1988). *The Culture of Terrorism*. Boston, MA: South End Press.

———. (1993). *Year 501: The Conquest Continues*. Boston, MA: South End Press.

Freire, Paulo. (1970). *Pedagogy of the Oppressed*. Translated by Myra Bergman Ramos. New York, NY: Herder & Herder.

———. (1973). *Education for Critical Consciousness*. New York, NY: Continuum.

Galtung, Johan. (1989). *Solving Conflicts: A Peace Research Perspective*. Honolulu, HI: University of Hawaii Institute for Peace.

Herman, Edward S., and Noam Chomsky (1988). *Manufacturing Consent: The Political Economy of the Mass Media*. New York, NY: Pantheon Books.

National Conference of Catholic Bishops. (1983). *The Challenge of Peace: God's Promise and Our Response. A Pastoral Letter on War and Peace, May 3, 1983*. Washington, DC: United States Catholic Conference.

Questions for Students Who Tutor as Part of the "Urban Dip"

Tutoring is a serious commitment. If you volunteer to tutor, we expect that you will meet your commitment throughout the semester. After you choose to tutor, but before your first day of tutoring, write and turn in to me about a page answering these questions:

1. Why did you choose tutoring as your urban dip option?
2. What do you think it will be like? What kind of people and situations do you expect to see? Where did you get these expectations? e.g. family, church, media, life experiences -- describe them.)
3. Do other people have different views than you do about the poor? What are they?

You should keep a journal of your tutoring experience, and write a report at the end of the semester. I would like to read your tutoring journal a couple of times during the semester.

For your final report, you will answer the questions listed here:

General observations:

1. Where did you tutor?
2. Referring back to the initial report in which you described your expectations, how did your experience agree with those expectations? How was it different?
3. Think back to your own experience in school when you were at the age of those you tutored or in their grade level, and answer:
   - How were you and your friends *like* the students you tutored? How were you *different?*
   - How were your school/neighborhood *like* the school/neighborhood where you tutored? How were they *different?*
4. What was the most difficult experience you had tutoring? How did you feel about it? How did you cope with it?
5. What was the most rewarding experience you had? How did it make you feel?
6. What was the funniest experience you had?

In relation to this class:

7. In what ways have your students' cultural background led them to react differently than you are used to? For example: eye contact, personal distance, things they consider funny.
8. (Effects and signs of conflict: oppression and militarization) Do you see any signs that your students are experiencing discrimination in or outside of school? Have you heard them reacting to the O.J. Simpson trials and the allegations against the Los Angeles police department? What attitudes do they have toward the local Twin Cities police and the school authorities?
9. (Descriptive analysis) What has led up to the school and neighborhood conditions your students live in, and what are the major causes of the conflicts they experience?
10. (Media) Have you learned anything about the world of your students that you would not have learned about through main-line media? What?
11. (Normative analysis: a utopia) What would a utopia look like for your school? What barriers stand in the way of realizing it?
12. (Action possibilities) What realistic hopes might one have for a better situation in your school and its neighborhood? What actions might move from the present situation toward that realistic better situation?

Feel free to comment on any other connections you notice between your tutoring experience and this class.

Final results of the experience:

13. How did your tutoring influence you? Did it change your understanding, opinions, and feelings in any way? Be specific.

Student Contributions to Public Life:
Peace and Justice Studies at the University of San Francisco

by Anne R. Roschelle, Jennifer Turpin, and Robert Elias

At the University of San Francisco (USF), as at many other colleges and universities around the country, we have become increasingly interested in preparing students for life outside the academy. Our university seeks to develop good citizens who will promote positive social values and participate fully in the democratic process. To contribute to this goal, faculty in the Peace and Justice Studies program (PJS) work to involve students in their local communities.

The PJS program was started in 1989 when Robert Elias joined the Politics faculty at USF. Having founded the peace studies program at Tufts University, Elias recognized the need for such a program at USF and its fit with the Jesuit mission of social justice. The program offers an interdisciplinary certificate in peace and justice studies and draws from courses in the departments of Politics, Sociology, Religious Studies, Philosophy, History, Economics, Communications, and Health. Some of these courses also meet requirements for certificates in women's studies, legal studies, ethnic studies, and other degree programs at the university. The PJS program currently has 50 students enrolled, with 12 core faculty and 18 affiliated faculty.

All students enrolled in PJS must complete five core courses, one elective, and a culminating fieldwork course in either the Politics department or the Sociology department. One core course must be selected from each of these categories: peace and war; global conflict resolution; human rights, repression, and violence; economic justice and development; and global movements and change.

The mission of the PJS program is to help students understand the broader context of social reality and their potential for promoting positive social change. Students are introduced to the possibility of change as evidenced by the unexpected end to the Cold War and the transformations in Eastern Europe as well as in other parts of the world (Elias and Turpin 1994). Reading assignments critically examine the paradox of living in a time of great potential and change while repression, militarism, and other forms of violence nevertheless persist, from the proliferation of nuclear weapons to the growth of ethnic, racial, and nationalist violence (Turpin and Kurtz 1997; Turpin and Lorentzen 1996). Students examine the widening gap between rich and poor nations (and the gap between the rich and poor in the richer nations) and the accompanying rise in disease, malnutrition, homelessness, infant mortality, and other forms of premature death. All of these issues and others are explored in depth through lectures, readings, and writing assignments.

In PJS we want to empower students to be active agents of social change. Thus, we analyze the relationships between conflict and change; we study global social movements, revolutions, and the changing currents of popular participation. Students learn how ordinary people, together with grass-roots leaders, have reshaped societies. We compare domestic participation (e.g., the women's and civil rights movements), activism abroad (e.g., the South African ANC and Sri Lankan Sarvodaya movements), and transnational actions (e.g., the human rights and anti-intervention movements). We assess the impact of liberation philosophies and of various religious and cultural movements. Through all of these, we seek to provide students with models of social change.

Features of the Service-Learning Courses

The Fieldwork course, taken in either politics or sociology, is the required service-learning course in PJS. Field placements are supervised by Jennifer Turpin (sociology) and Robert Elias (politics), who have created an extensive database of Bay Area social service organizations. Students select several sites of interest from the database after consulting with these professors. After visiting each site, students choose their placement and commit to at least 25 hours of service per unit of course credit.

The course provides skill-building opportunities and helps students integrate peace and justice theories with concrete practice. Students read several texts that address issues of peace and justice as well as social and political participation (e.g., Driver 1992; Shaw 1996). Students also read books related specifically to the population they are serving.

Students often go through different developmental stages during their service work and sometimes need help sorting out their feelings, some of which can be intense. Stereotypes may be reinforced, or students may resent the population they are serving. They may begin with such initial enthusiasm that they burn out too fast. The faculty conduct either weekly or biweekly group discussion sessions that address these issues. There are both structured and less formal reflection opportunities to connect students' service work to the academic literature as well as to help them examine the evolution of their thoughts and emotions throughout the semester.

Students keep a weekly fieldwork journal that documents their community service and provides an opportunity to assess and evaluate their work systematically. They discuss in detail their experiences, their views of the population they are serving, whether or not stereotypes are being rein-forced, and how their experience connects to the required reading and the larger social structure. Students are also encouraged to reflect upon how the clients are responding to their service work. Students sometimes expect the population they are serving to be grateful. When it is not, they may feel resentful. Students are asked to consider how service work is socially con-structed. They are challenged to question their motives for helping and to trace the development of these feelings throughout the semester.

Faculty guide students in applying academic concepts to their commu-nity work and in pursuing a deeper understanding of the implications of that work (Hondagneu-Sotelo and Raskoff 1994). Placing students in a ser-vice role and providing them with the opportunity to reflect on the struc-tural causes of inequality is especially important in lessening the danger that their participation will help reinforce an unjust system (Schultz 1990). Students are challenged to consider how they can promote social change within the constraints of a social structure that oftentimes seems ominous and static.

A PJS Elective Service-Learning Course

One of the PJS course electives also requires service-learning. In Poverty, Homelessness and the Urban Underclass, taught by Anne Roschelle, stu-dents must complete at least 30 hours of service. Placements are made through USF's Office of Community Service and Service Learning. Students are required to fill out a weekly service report, indicating their hours of work and specific responsibilities. In addition, at the end of the semester, place-ment supervisors write a final report about the student's performance.

The course seeks to help students understand how the social structure affects different individuals in American society. It emphasizes the structur-al and economic transformations in the U.S. production economy and their effects on the urban poor. In addition, reading assignments examine the dif-ferential impact of economic disenfranchisement on various racial, ethnic, and gender groups (Roschelle 1997). Required readings help students exam-ine theoretical perspectives that explain poverty's persistence. Students are encouraged to evaluate whether or not the theories adequately reflect the reality of the disenfranchised individuals with whom they work.

In order to maximize the community responsibility emphasis, students are grouped based on their community service placements and are required to collaborate to produce a policy paper. Members of each group determine how to divide the workload and what specific policy issue to emphasize. Each final paper includes a discussion of the social structural antecedents of poverty, an analysis of an existing program targeted at the population the group members are serving, an evaluation of that program's limitations, and policy recommendations for eradicating inequality among their target population. At the end of the semester, students present their policy papers to the organizations they served. Rather than the service hours representing a percentage of the final grade, the service component is integrated into the reflection and policy paper.

Several minor problems have been encountered in the Fieldwork and Poverty, Homelessness and the Urban Underclass courses. Many students have not started their service work until several weeks into the semester and thus have completed fewer hours than required. Some students have been assigned mainly clerical duties. Some have resented either the actual service or the population they were serving; others had their stereotypes reinforced. We recommend that faculty require students to initiate service within the first two weeks of the semester and that faculty determine which sites offer the most appropriate hands-on experience.

Despite such obstacles, service-learning plays an important role in the Peace and Justice Studies program. Although we encourage the expansion of service-learning in all our courses, some limitations must be acknowledged. Many of our faculty are new to the Bay Area, and unless they are doing community-based research, they remain unfamiliar with community service agencies. As is common in universities, faculty face pressures to teach, publish, and do service, and have little time left to introduce innovations such as service-learning in the classroom. Although there is a service-learning office at USF, reflecting the administration's support for this pedagogy, for a variety of reasons few faculty access its resources.

Students are also limited in the number of service-learning courses they can take. Students who work part- or full-time, enroll in five classes per semester, and want to have social lives, find the logistics of multiple community service responsibilities to be both physically and psychologically difficult.

Student Impact on Community Service Organizations

Much of the research on service-learning examines the impact of that learning on students and their intellectual and personal growth, focusing in particular on the community's usefulness in promoting greater academic understanding (see, for example, Kuhn 1995 and Parker-Gwin 1996). But very little has been written about the impact students have on the organizations they serve (for an exception, see Calderon and Farrell 1996). By using examples from student field papers and field journals, we can illustrate how, through service-learning, students at USF have positively influenced the local community.

Because of their exposure to the Jesuit tradition at USF and their involvement in courses that offer analyses of race, class, gender, and nation, students often bring ideals of multiculturalism, social justice, and conflict resolution to the organizations they serve and thus make a helpful contribution to the agency. Environmental groups, for example, have failed sometimes to reflect the concerns of politically and economically disenfranchised individuals throughout the world. The discourse of U.S. environmental movements at times conceptualizes conservation in terms of jobs versus animal and environmental protection. This approach can marginalize concerns about environmental racism or global economic development. We seek to provide PJS students with the necessary tools to develop a more holistic approach to environmental protection and to educate activists about alternative perspectives. They have done so, for example, in environmental groups focusing on recycling and coastal cleanups.

Such initiatives have also helped create a more positive relationship between the community and the university. Having students work in organizations such as Oxfam, Greenpeace, Amnesty International, the American Civil Liberties Union, the National Association for the Advancement of Colored People, and in homeless and battered women's shelters, soup kitchens, and other human rights groups has improved the university's reputation for social service.

Service-learning students have also brought nationally recognized guest speakers to campus and have sponsored film series. Some have continued their service work after they completed their service-learning courses and the PJS program. Many students go above and beyond the requirements of their fieldwork placements to create a lasting effect on the organizations they serve. In one case, a student conducted diversity training workshops for new volunteers at her service-learning site; the success of these workshops led the program director to implement permanent student-run diversity training workshops. Another student helped institute inservice workshops on sexism and sexual harassment in the educational program in which she was an intern. One student organized and conducted workshops on domestic violence for women at several homeless shelters around the Bay Area; as a result, this student ended up providing advice and social service referrals that concretely helped some women escape from their violent relationships.

Another student, working with the San Francisco Women's Foundation, wrote a policy manual about the lack of domestic abuse services for immigrant women; as a result, she was appointed to serve on a Bay Area commission on violence against women, working with attorneys, policymakers, and professional organizers. Other students have written a comprehensive organizer's manual; planned and implemented a conference on alternative development policies; and initiated a new referral service for health-care rights for Latino immigrants. In these and many other cases, students contributed something unique that their organizations probably would not have had the resources to have instituted on their own.

Conclusion

Students both learn from the groups they encounter in their service work and also positively affect the programs they serve. Not only do many students continue to serve after the course ends, but many also seek careers in public service as a result. Students who have completed the courses and programs work for the Peace Corps, the Jesuit Volunteer Corps, and Teach For America. Others have taken jobs with public officials, social service agencies, and advocacy groups.

Still other students have enrolled in law school and graduate programs emphasizing peace and social justice issues, and they have become public-interest lawyers, social workers, and policy advocates. In different ways and through different avenues, veterans of service-learning contribute to public life both during and beyond their years at USF and their participation in the Peace and Justice Studies program.

References

Calderon, J., and B. Farrell. (1996). "Doing Sociology: Connecting the Classroom Experience With a Multiethnic School District." *Teaching Sociology* 26: 46-53.

Driver, D. (1992). *Defending the Left: An Individual's Guide to Fighting for Social Justice, Individual Rights, and the Environment.* Chicago, IL: Noble Press.

Elias, R., and J. Turpin. (1994). *Rethinking Peace.* Boulder, CO: Lynne Rienner.

Hondagneu-Sotelo, P., and S. Raskoff. (1994). "Community Service-Learning: Promises and Problems." *Teaching Sociology* 22: 248-254.

Kuhn, G.D. (1995). "The Other Curriculum: Out-of-Class Experiences Associated With Student Learning and Personal Development." *Journal of Higher Education* 66(2): 123-155.

Parker-Gwin, R. (1996). "Connecting Service to Learning: How Students and Communities Matter." *Teaching Sociology* 24: 97-101.

Roschelle, A. (1997). *No More Kin: Exploring Race, Class, and Gender in Family Networks.* New York, NY, and London: Sage Publications.

Schultz, S.K. (1990). "From Isolation to Commitment: The Role of the Community in Values Education." *New Directions for Student Services* 50: 91-100.

Shaw, R. (1996). *The Activist's Handbook: A Guide for the 1990's.* Berkeley, CA: University of California Press.

Turpin, J., and L.A. Lorentzen. (1996). *The Gendered New World Order: Militarism, Development, and the Environment.* New York, NY: Routledge.

Turpin, J., and L.R. Kurtz. (1997). *The Web of Violence: From Interpersonal to Global.* Urbana, IL: University of Illinois Press.

Peace Building Through Foreign Study in Northern Ireland: The Earlham College Example

by Anthony Bing

In *The Ways of Peace: A Philosophy of Peace as Action,* a book that should be assigned reading in every peace studies curriculum, author Gray Cox (1986: 9) notes that "peace," unlike "war," is not used as a verb:

> We think of war as an activity in which people can purposely engage. It is something soldiers can learn how to do. In contrast, we think of peace as a kind of condition or state which is achieved or simply occurs. Unlike warring, peace is not thought to be something to <u>do</u>.

In creating a philosophy of peace as action, and in opening ways for those wishing to experience peace through participating in its creation, Cox (1986: 19) observes that "so far as the international scene goes, there is no other way to peace except the peace that is a way." Learning about peace by learning how to be peacemakers is one of the goals of the Earlham College Peace Studies Program in Northern Ireland. Through important experiential components, including homestays, reflective ethnographic journals, and especially field placements with agencies promoting social change in Northern Ireland, Earlham students learn how being both observers and participants in a culture of conflict offers important insights into what might constitute a culture of peace.

To learn how we may come to an understanding of a process "defined not by conflicts that define oppositions but by problems that pose difficulties," Cox (1986: 13) maintains that we must go beyond our culture's fondness for "eristic" reasoning. Such reasoning, with its "rhetoric rich with metaphors of physical combat and war" (1986: 33), defends positions, wins arguments, and outmaneuvers opponents, thus contributing to what is called a culture of conflict. Instead, we must adopt "maieutic" reasoning, "a cooperative cultivating of shared insights" (1986: 36), which leads to and is characteristic of a culture of peace. Indeed, when maieutic reasoning exists, the conditions of a peace culture exist, for this reasoning leads to a "process of agreeing — the cultivation of a shared commitment to common expressions, projects and practices" (1986: 127).

Maieutic is a word rich in connotations. Derived from the Greek *maieusis,* meaning "midwifery," the word suggests that truth emerges like the birth of a child, as a cooperative effort of midwife and mother, so that "truth is an overall characteristic of emergent networks of insights and perceptions of fact in their various relations" (1986: 36-37). Unlike eristic reasoning, which is detached and disinterested and refers to a fixed reality, in maieutic reasoning "feeling is viewed as continuous with reason. Emotions are viewed as cognitive in character" (1986: 37). Truth is not fixed in an a priori fashion, but is emergent in particular contexts. Maieutic reasoning, in Cox's view, leads us to "view differences between people as aspects of shared problems rather than oppositions between competitors" (1986: 64).

Earlham College Peace Studies Program in Northern Ireland

The goal of Earlham's Peace Studies Program in Northern Ireland is to offer students an experience in maieutic reasoning, in learning to value the connection of emotion and thought, theory, and practice, by participating in the process of bringing forth new conditions, establishing new ways of looking at human differences, and fostering insights into what it would mean to replace a culture of conflict with a culture of peace.

Earlham's International Programs Office has introduced service-learning elements into its philosophy of off-campus study. In the international study programs with a peace studies focus, Jerusalem and Northern Ireland in particular, participation in a culture through understanding how it attempts to create peace from conflict involves students in a process of cultural transformation whose implications are global in scope. This interaction goes beyond a vague sense of mutuality where everyone "takes something from the experience." The peace studies dimension expands the scope of service and off-campus study when a student finds herself or himself participating in forming both a local and a global community of peace. For our students, these experiences have ranged from working in a Cuatla, Mexico, environmental organization, to working in a center for differently abled children in Bogota, Colombia, to working in a women's weaving cooperative in Kaimosi, Kenya, to teaching in integrated primary and secondary schools in Northern Ireland.

Before examining in detail how peace studies intersects with service-learning, a brief description of the Northern Ireland program is in order.[1] The goal of the program is to increase students' understanding of the complexities of the conflict in Northern Ireland and to use this knowledge to increase their understanding of conflict in their own and other societies. Although the program is open to students in every discipline, we hope that, for the Peace and Global Studies majors in particular, this understanding of the conflict will be accompanied by an awareness of what it takes to transform a culture of conflict to a culture of peace.

About 8 to 14 students spend an extended semester in Northern Ireland, largely in Londonderry/Derry and Belfast, which is preceded by an orientation at Earlham the previous semester. At this time, Mervyn Love, the program's resident director, indicates to the students which service opportunities he has prepared for the following semester and asks them to be prepared to tell him as soon as they arrive, and preferably before they arrive, which placements they desire. He also tries to accommodate students interested in experiences other than the ones on his list, and when he returns to Ireland, he initiates contacts with organizations that might meet the students' interests. As the students arrive in Londonderry/Derry, they receive an orientation at their field placement site, and this is followed by about 11 weeks of classes at the Magee campus of the University of Ulster. During this period, the students spend one day a week in field placements.

Following a week's trip to Dublin, the students take up residence in Belfast, where they continue their coursework and devote four full days a week to their field placements. The program includes two residential weekends during which the students meet with Love to evaluate their experiences and to reflect upon them. During the initial period in Londonderry/Derry the students live with Protestant and Catholic families and attend classes especially designed for them at Magee College. Three of their courses help them put the Northern Ireland conflict in context. These are The History and Background to the Troubles, The Government and Politics of Northern Ireland, and International Conflict Resolution — A Study of Northern Ireland. In addition to these courses, which are completed during the students' stay in Londonderry/Derry, the students begin two semester-spanning courses that most closely coordinate with their field placement and housing experiences. The first course, Peace Building Through Reconciliation, is taught by Love and is described as

> a general introduction [to] and discussion on the different meanings of reconciliation, defining some important terms; e.g., stereotyping, prejudice, scapegoating, alienation, polarization, conflict and violence, conflict resolution and conciliation. The class includes seminar meetings with speakers from all of the political parties in Northern Ireland, a field trip to meet security forces and meetings with religious and community leaders.

A second course, Conflict and Identity, taught by Derick Wilson and Duncan Morrow, is described as

> an introduction to law and order in divided societies. Seminars focus on such topics as "Sharing a Place," "Change, Stability, and Security," "Experiences of Rituals and Conflict," "Symbols I Love and Despise," "Experiences of Change," "My Scapegoats, Politeness and Avoidance," "Difference and Diversity," "Transcendence, Different Approaches in Different Places," "Identity Now for Me." The final weeks in Belfast are used to relate and integrate placement work into the theoretical ideas talked about in this class.

Conflict and Identity: Peace Studies and Service-Learning

Conflict and Identity is the course that most closely illustrates the intersection of service-learning and peace studies. This course, tied closely to a sense of maieutic reasoning about the nature of a truth that emerges from experience, encourages each student to explore and discover her or his own identity and the conflict that may accompany it. The instructors place special emphasis on what is going on for the student at that particular time in the context of living in Northern Ireland, being with a family, and working with an agency. Important questions addressed in the context of the course include: How does the student learn to ask questions without giving offense? How can the student make connections between what has and is being taught at the theoretical level and what the student is experiencing in the workplace or in the living situation? Students leave Northern Ireland believing that this course is indispensable to clarifying and pulling together their total experience.

The supervised field placement is the site of the service that is integrated into the academic program. In this placement the student is given an opportunity to work directly with the people of Northern Ireland and to learn about the issues the people deal with on a daily basis. Students are in direct contact with both sides of the conflict by being placed in organizations that work with both Catholics and Protestants.

Each student meets with his or her agency to agree upon his or her duties. The student carries through with the agreed-upon work under the supervision of someone in the agency, although Love visits students during the placements and consults with agency supervisors about progress and, at times, problems. At the end of the placement each supervisor prepares an evaluation of her or his student's work, after first receiving that student's self-evaluation. The placements are evaluated on a pass/fail basis, though the experiences and the reflections on them enter into the grade given in the Conflict and Identity course. As noted earlier, placements provide material for discussion in both this course and the Peace Building Through Reconciliation course.

In each agency the students are asked to accomplish the following:

(1) Understand the agency and its mission.

(2) Know the staff and what they do and why.

(3) Understand the place of the agency in the context of the wider community in Northern Ireland.

(4) Understand the agency's history and previous contributions to the wider community.

(5) Know how the wider community regards the agency and why.

(6) Undertake a piece of work for the agency.

It is interesting to compare these six tasks with the new kind of social research Cox claims is necessary for constructing a culture of peace:

> To understand people we must (1) learn how their own network of holistic meanings provides a context (2) that they take to give them reasons which justify their action (3) in terms of value-laden notions (4) and normative institutions that — unlike the laws of nature — can be revised. The fifth point is that our understanding of these requires participation. To see how they understand their own activity, we cannot just peek at them for a moment. We must enter into their social world as they conceive it. (1986: 72)

Service-Learning in One Student's Experience: An example of one student's Belfast placement reveals quite clearly how the Northern Ireland program fosters this new kind of social research and shows in an engaging way not only the benefits derived from participation in service-learning but also the emergent nature of the truth that one carries away from it. The student in question was placed in an agency that was divided physically by the "peace wall" separating the Catholic and Protestant communities in Belfast. Its physical location was the scene of some of the most brutal violence in Northern Ireland. The student was able to accomplish the first five steps in her agency, but when she came to the sixth, "undertaking a piece of work for the agency," she was initially frustrated. She was eager to be given "hands-on" work that could unite the two communities. Throughout the semester she had been dreaming of, in her terms, "doing something positive" for the two communities she had come to care for. The reluctance of her agency to provide her immediately with such an opportunity caused her to look more deeply into the situation, giving up some fixed notions she had about reconciliation and her role in it, and allowing her to see the truth as it emerged from the situation; namely, that the two communities were unequally prepared for positive cross-cultural encounters. Her self-evaluation of her placement performance not only reflects Cox's five points but also shows her own move from naïveté to maturity without a loss of the idealism and optimism necessary for anyone who would become a peacemaker. The following is taken from her self-evaluation:

> (1) My placement knew I had to get to know the staff, the area and the communities so they made me shadow the workers and ask questions. [I had to go] to lots of meetings and conferences and walk around the area.

> (2) [I had to analyze] what they were doing and why.

> (3) I now understand that one of the communities is NOT ready for any sort of cross-community encounter — it's too early.

(4) *The work that is required in one community is about "single identity."*

(5) *One community already has structures and lots of community projects, but the other hasn't reached that far yet and it needs help.*

(6) *Until each of the communities is comfortable with their identity then it will not be reasonable to do large cross-community work schemes.*

(7) *I am now beginning my work with a Protestant youth group to try and help them discover who they are and where they want to be.*

(8) *It's important for the leaders and workers of the projects to work cross-community and keep their links open, but it is too early for the Protestant community in this area to engage in cross- or inter-community work.*

(9) *My contribution will be to help this process and take back to the USA a greater understanding of the complexities and difficulties of the two communities trying to work together.*

Love's assessment of the student's experience reveals the sort of maieutic reasoning present in the student's assessment of her experience:

This student has seen that although she may not have had wonderful opportunities to "save" the situation and bring two opposing communities together, she has come from an "idealized" goal to analyze the reality of the situation. She has gone further in that she has accepted that this is for the people of the area to decide, so you have to listen to them, attempt to understand them, and move at their pace.

Clearly the student is learning what it takes to create a culture of peace. In the words of Cox:

The moral to draw here is that we can keep a more accurate perspective on what peace involves if we do not think of it as a thing that we make or a state that we reach but conceive of it as a process we undertake. It is an activity in which we engage. It is not a position to be adopted but a movement along a vector. It is a process of agreeing — the cultivation of a shared commitment to common expressions, projects, and practices. (1986: 127)

Peace Studies and Service-Learning

It is now time to see how this sort of international experience fits into a common understanding of service-learning. The Northern Ireland program, with its academic focus on the conflict there, with its structure that stresses the connection of theory and practice, and with its impact on the lives of students engaged in the process of understanding that conflict, clearly incorporates most of the goals of service-learning as defined in this monograph.

What is critical, however, is to spell out what is meant by "meeting the needs of a community." At first glance, it may seem that the Northern Ireland program (and most other foreign study programs) serves almost exclusively the needs of participating students. Most communities are not asked whether they would like foreign students to meet their needs, but rather consent to serve as laboratories for the students to test out theories about peace building and social transformation that students then take back to their own countries. Indeed, one would have to admit that in our Northern Ireland program most of the benefits go to the students. As Love states,

> The learning is complex. It involves listening and understanding, analyzing, checking out, determining the best way forward, setting agreed aims and goals, weaving together the various strands of academic theory, practice and life. Sometimes this may involve service directly to the agency and thus indirectly to the wider community, but the primary benefit is to developing the understanding of the student and his or her ability to learn from the situation in the hopes that they can extrapolate this and use the knowledge gained positively back home.

It would, in fact, be presumptuous and perhaps bordering on cultural imperialism to suppose that Earlham students have a lot to offer to the resolution of the conflict in Northern Ireland. Nonetheless, to the extent that students become participants in the reconciliation process, they do "serve" the communities.

There is, however, another aspect of the ways in which students interact with the agencies of their field placements that helps deepen the notion of "service" and "meeting the needs of a community." Cox points out that understanding another culture is a necessary but not sufficient step toward creating a culture of peace. *Critical* understanding is also necessary, and in providing this our students may be of more service to communities in conflict than they at first realize. Cox observes that most people's self-understanding is always vague and implicit to some degree. If this is so, our students as researchers can fulfill an important function in asking agencies to define their goals and objectives and to relate the history of their successes and failures. This questioning becomes joint in character in that an answer by the agency involves it in the process of questioning.

> The joint character of the inquiry bears emphasis. Each brings something distinctive to it. The subject brings the activity to be understood. The researcher brings a new or different perspective which raises questions the subject might never have asked or which suggests answers the subject might not have thought of proposing. . . . This means that in normal cases

the researcher and the people she studies are related to each other not as a manipulator to a group of things of "objects" but as one subject to another subject, as I to thou — as participants in a dialogue. And it is a dialogue which in its own limited way provides a paradigm of peace-making. For here human differences are conceived of not as latent conflicts between people with opposed interests but as shared problems to be resolved in mutual agreement. (Cox 1986: 82-83)

Cox's words, when coupled with the above description of the Northern Ireland field placements, show the intersection of peace studies and service-learning in a very clear fashion.

I should add that there are other ways our students "serve" the agencies that go beyond an explanation of goals and objectives. In some cases our students have actually used their experiences in the United States to illuminate and bring new perspectives to some situations. Thus, a Jewish student, sensitive to discrimination that goes beyond the confessional divisions in Northern Ireland, pointed out to one agency how a Chinese woman was being discriminated against by children in the project. The adults in her center, focused so completely on Protestant-Catholic divisions in their community, were oblivious to the Chinese woman's plight. Another student, working in an environmental educational program in Ireland, was able to use her background in outdoor education, environmental studies, and sustainable agriculture to help institute a paper recycling project for fifth graders in Belfast. And one should not minimize the new energy the students bring to the agencies that have opened their doors to them. Nonetheless, it is probably a healthy sign that in their reflective sessions with Love, Wilson, and Morrow, most students do not say a lot about what they were able to contribute.

What Cox wrote is still sadly true:

We live in a culture in which predominant conceptions of reason, feeling, meaning, value, truth, and the self characterize activity in terms of conflict, and this view is buttressed by conceptions of knowledge and action which are entrenched in the dominant institutions of our society. We find it difficult to conceive of human activity in ways which do not make conflict an essential feature of it. In this sense, we live in a culture of conflict, and, for us, it remains difficult to conceive of peace in any other way than as a static absence. (1986: 61)

It is the goal of the academic study of peace to help people conceive of peace as an activity, not a static absence. One of the great accomplishments of the Northern Ireland program is that our students learn through their participation in that culture that peace is an activity. Although all returning students are saddened that peace and reconciliation have not yet been achieved there, nor for that matter in the United States, they have become convinced that it is possible. This learning is crucial for those who would be peacemakers and who would meet service-learning's goal of "civic responsibility" in its fullest possible sense.

Note

1. Much of this description has been furnished by Mervyn Love, one of the program's chief architects and its resident director since its inception in 1991.

Reference

Cox, Gray. (1986). *The Ways of Peace: A Philosophy of Peace as Action.* New York, NY: Paulist Press.

The International and National Voluntary Service Training Program (INVST) at the University of Colorado at Boulder

by James R. Scarritt and Seana Lowe

A group of University of Colorado at Boulder faculty, staff, and students met in the fall of 1989 to take a hard look at undergraduate education. The group concluded that students were not being adequately prepared for the challenges of the 21st century, which included solving the problems of environmental degradation, failing schools, resource depletion, poverty, racial and ethnic conflict, violence, and social inequality and injustice. A curriculum was needed that would equip students with the theoretical and practical skills to meet those challenges in a creative, sensitive, and mature way.

In the summer of 1990, the International and National Voluntary Service Training program (INVST), a two-year academic and service-learning leadership training program designed for juniors and seniors, enrolled its first cohort of 15 students at the University of Colorado at Boulder. Currently, 25 students are in the program. Based on the pedagogy of service-learning, the program offers a unique educational experience to students of all majors through the combination of a 16-credit academic program of small, innovative classes, two noncredit summer programs of community service in the United States and abroad, and community service — usually in the Boulder-Denver area — during the fall and spring semesters. The program combines academic and service perspectives on the issues of global development, nonviolent social change, interpersonal conflict and conflict resolution, and community development, focusing especially on poverty, racism, and other manifestations of social inequality and injustice. Students make a commitment to do at least two years of community service following graduation. A special feature of the program is that it provides a wide-ranging combination of academic and practical experiences to college students with a focus on nonviolent social change.

Overview of the INVST Program

The program's general mission is ambitious but sound: *To develop well-informed citizens who are trained as leaders to analyze and solve community problems as a lifetime commitment.* INVST emphasizes the interaction between theory and practice, with the following goals for students:

(1) To learn the basis of community; (2) To develop critical analysis skills by looking at the structural causes of social and environmental problems; (3) To develop empathetic understanding of those who are oppressed; (4) To learn to work with people, not for people, in a reciprocal relationship of mutual benefit and inter-cultural exchange; (5) To develop a sense of personal responsibility by seeing that individual actions and inactions affect social structures (the personal is political); *(6) To develop understanding regarding the connections between social and environmental communities* (the environmental is social); *(7) To develop understanding regarding the interdependence among nations in creating and solving problems [that] are global in nature; (8) To develop community leadership skills; (9) To develop organizational skills; (10) To explore personal attitudes and beliefs about community, community development, sexism, racism, heterosexism, classism, and other contemporary social issues; (11) To understand how people counter violence with non-violent action; (12) To explore personal and community visions of social change in order to facilitate post-graduate direction and placement as community leaders.*

To realize its goals, INVST includes four 3-credit courses, four 1-credit lab practica, and two month-long summer programs. In addition, students serve an average of six hours a week with community service organizations during their first academic year, and in "Community SOL" (Service, Organization, and Leadership) projects during their second academic year. The four classes are specifically designed to train students for leadership in community service, and all of them address peace studies issues. These are small, innovative classes that encourage student involvement and that strive for a balance between intellectual reflection and community action. The sequence of courses and experiences moves from exploring interpersonal relations to microsocial issues to macrosocial issues. Typically, the courses lay the theoretical foundations that are integrated with the summer service experiences, while the practica teach organizational and leadership skills that are applied in the service experiences during the academic year.

First Year of the Program

The first intensive summer program includes an orientation to INVST, a one-week wilderness experience, a week working with the homeless in Denver, and two weeks living and serving with Native Americans of the Dineh (Navajo) Nation. Throughout the month, students are assigned readings and are guided in journal reflection and integrative discussions. The orientation covers topics that facilitate participation in INVST such as (1) an overview of the philosophy of service-learning, (2) a discussion of the program's design and assumptions, (3) training in communication and listening skills, and (4) multicultural training.

The wilderness experience is designed to develop community and to teach basic survival skills. Students begin to understand the interdependence between social and environmental communities. In addition, this experience provides students with opportunities to learn interpersonal skills that will help them adapt to different situations and to be effective as members of a group. These skills are necessary for their subsequent service projects, for their two years together in the INVST program, and for their community service after graduation.

The students then go to the Samaritan House homeless shelter in Denver where they (1) learn about homelessness for two days; (2) visit a variety of organizations providing shelter, food, and medical services to the homeless; and (3) serve in one of these organizations. Samaritan House, generally considered to be one of the best homeless shelters in the country, is superbly equipped to provide valuable training for our students in exchange for their service.

Next, students work on community projects in the Dineh Nation. By living with the Dineh people and serving with them by clearing fields, determining and charting water tables, doing construction work, and participating in other community projects and rituals, the students get a firsthand look at another culture and its unique challenges. Students also are trained in permaculture, the practice of sustainable agriculture. Preparation for this experience includes select readings about the Dineh, multicultural training, and presentations by Native Americans.

In the fall semester of the first year, INVST students take Facilitating Peaceful Community Change and the associated practicum. The aim is to provide knowledge and skills that will enable students to become more effective organizers and facilitators of community efforts toward social change. The course focuses on communication, collaboration, power, multicultural issues, and community building. Students gain theoretical knowledge and practical skills about how to work with others in solving community problems, how to mediate conflicts, and how to facilitate meetings. In the first part of the course, the focus is on giving students a better understanding of their own ways of processing knowledge ("cognitive maps") and their culture, and on the ways in which these affect their thinking. In the second part, the focus is on the interpersonal understanding and skills needed for social change facilitators, and on how groups, communities, and organizations develop and function effectively.

In the following semester, students take Implementing Social Change and the associated practicum, which involves active research analyzing community needs and proposing solutions. The focus is on theories and techniques of the change process. Cooperative learning activities are emphasized. Using case studies of community change from the United States and abroad, students learn how social problems have been solved and are currently being addressed in many different communities. This comprehensive examination of change gives them valuable information about how the change process comes about and what leadership skills are essential for it to be effective. Assignments include analysis of a service sector (social services, education, health, planning, and others) and diagnosis of a community problem as well as approaches to solving it. Practical skills such as writing grant proposals and giving public presentations also are developed.

During the first year, each INVST student works as an "Intern Plus" under the close supervision of a staff member at a local service organization. The Intern Plus service-learning placement is an opportunity for students to develop organizational and community leadership skills while serving in a reciprocal relationship with a local community service organization. Students fulfill agency and community needs, attend staff meetings, meet regularly with their supervisors, and work on specified skills. Integration and guided reflection on the service experiences occur in the first-year practica.

The assistant director assumes responsibility for ensuring that the students' performance meets program expectations and the standards of the service agencies. After a month-long informational interview process, students and supervisors select each other for the academic year. The commitment begins with their completing a "confirmation of commitment" that identifies mutual expectations for the service experience and solidifies a new or continuing relationship between INVST and the community agency. An evaluation of each student's efforts and impact is completed by that agency at the end of each semester.

Second Year of the Program

The second summer program provides students with a global perspective by giving them the opportunity to live in a foreign country. Traditionally, INVST classes have lived in the poor areas of Kingston, Jamaica, for one month. The students have served at such places as the Mustard Seed Orphanage and Community Development Center, Women's Media Watch, the Jamaican Forest Service, and the Red Cross. In 1996, the second-year class lived and served in Mexico. In preparation for their experiences abroad, the students read and discuss relevant materials and meet with experts on the host country. An experience in a developing country is essential for educating INVST students about the global scope of the problems they will confront while they are involved in community service leadership roles, as well as the practical problems of trying to apply solutions devised for one cultural context to another. Being in a developing country also gives students a better understanding of community problems in the United States by providing them with a comparative perspective.

In the first semester of the second year, INVST students take Democracy and Nonviolent Social Movements and the associated practicum. The course explores the relationship between democracy and nonviolent social movements around the world. Although the focus is primarily on nonviolent theory and action, arguments and methods of those who advocate violence are also considered. Questions that are addressed include: What is violence? What is nonviolence? Why do some groups seeking social change choose nonviolent rather than violent means? What do specific movements mean by "democracy"? Do they embody it or only seek it? How are their views on democracy related to their choice for or against violence or nonviolence? Special attention is given to leadership, grass-roots development, the issue of means and ends, decision-making processes, economic and ecological programs, and the decentralization of power.

The capstone course — taken in the students' final semester — is Critical Thinking on Development, which involves students in critical reflection on development at the local, national, and global levels. This course and the accompanying practicum provide them with a perspective on the underlying structural causes of social problems and explore different strategies for solving those problems. What the students have learned in other courses is placed in global economic, political, social, and cultural contexts. Students think critically about the ways in which these contexts constrain and/or facilitate change efforts. The course begins with an examination of various definitions of the term *development* and asks whether — defined in any of these ways — the term provides a useful means of conceptualizing the package of changes that INVST graduates have a lifetime commitment to facilitate. Through a critical examination of various models of development, students explore the major components of development, how they are interrelated, and how they can be modified or changed. The interrelationships among democratization, voluntary associations, and sustainable growth with equity are explored. Examples are drawn from the settings in which the students have had service-learning experiences.

Throughout the second academic year, students also work in teams on Community SOL projects, which provide them with an opportunity to design, implement, and evaluate their own community service initiatives. Students identify a community to be served, and in collaboration with members of the community, research needs and capacities in order to identify the goals and objectives of their particular projects. For example, during the 1995-96 academic year, one group of students declared their mission to be "to contribute to the development of global sustainability on a local level."

Working with the San Juan del Centro neighborhood and Community Food Share, they facilitated an organic gardening project by providing materials and assistance to diverse families interested in growing their own food. Upon completion of this Community SOL project, the San Juan del Centro neighborhood had nine garden plots being planted. This experience gives INVST students the opportunity to apply and further develop organizational and leadership skills while being engaged in meaningful community service. Critical analysis of and guided reflection on project experiences occur in the second-year practica.

Administration of the INVST Program

The INVST program is administered and constantly adjusted by the Directors' Committee, which is composed of the director, the associate director, the assistant director, the administrative coordinator, teaching faculty, and six student representatives. All meetings are facilitated by students, and all major policy decisions are reached through consensus. Student representatives meet regularly with the other students on issues before the Directors' Committee through their classes and practica, as well as through all-INVST meetings. The nine faculty, staff, and graduate students currently involved in the program are from political science, sociology, psychology, law, journalism, education, and the Counseling Services Multicultural Center. This group, known as the "INVST staff," meets periodically to discuss issues relating to the program and to make recommendations to the Directors' Committee. At the university level, our formal partnerships include the Service-Learning Center[1] and the Service-Learning Program Council, which share a commitment to promote service-learning on campus; the Farrand Residential Academic Program; and our "Associated Faculty," who are committed to the values of INVST.

Beyond its strong partnerships with the service-learning community at the university, INVST shares collaborative energy and support with an extensive group of community allies, including our partners in service and other local and national organizations committed to making a difference.

Impact of the INVST Program

The first INVST class of 11 students graduated in May 1992, the second class of 6 in 1993, the third class of 14 in 1994, the fourth class of 19 in 1995, and the fifth class of 12 in 1996. Many of those students are now pursuing careers in existing service organizations or are creating new service initiatives. Some examples of the organizations in which they are serving or have served include the Peace Corps, World Teach, Teach For America, the Corporation for National Service, Covenant House, the National Civilian Community Corps, Public Allies, Colorado Youth at Risk, Habitat for Humanity, the Colorado Conservation Fund, Boulder Valley Schools, and the Colorado Coalition for the Homeless. One of our recent graduates is chair of the Colorado State Commission on National and Community Service.

As reported by Myers-Lipton (1994: 147-219), the former assistant director of INVST, a number of important changes occur in INVST students as a result of their participation in the program: They develop a sense of civic responsibility, reduce their level of racial prejudice, and gain greater international understanding. One student summarized the impact of the program very well in his exit interview: "INVST has been a life-changing experience more shaping of my university years than my major . . . it's helped me live justly as a human being and an engaged citizen . . . translating my beliefs into a way of life that teaches by example."

INVST was initially designed exclusively as a training program and has achieved considerable success in that regard, as the preceding discussion of its impact demonstrates. However, we now realize that it is important for us to facilitate initial postgraduation placements for our students and to do what we can to assure that these initial placements will combine with our graduates' dedication, skills, and experience to produce well-informed citizens who have a lifetime commitment to the analysis and solution of community, national, and global problems. We have developed a comprehensive plan for addressing the specific and closely related issues involved in attaining these broad goals: career development, alumnae/i relations, and relations with community allies. Recently, an Information Resource Center has been established, using mainly volunteer labor. The INVST Alumnae/i Advisory Board is heavily involved in the program in a number of ways, including fundraising, production of a newsletter, and facilitation of summer experiences.

INVST and Peace Studies

INVST is intended to connect the theoretical and substantive concerns of peace studies, leadership training, and the pedagogy of service-learning. In fact, students completing the INVST program and three additional courses, including the introductory course and Senior Seminar (both in peace and conflict studies), are eligible to receive a certificate in peace and conflict studies from the university. All INVST courses are truly interdisciplinary or, more accurately, transdisciplinary (Stephenson 1989: 9; Rank 1989: 89). The curriculum does not give much emphasis to war or negative peace but deals substantially with virtually all other areas of peace studies, including nonviolence, social movements, conflict resolution, economic justice, human rights, and ecological balance (Lopez 1989: 76). It analyzes these at all levels, from the individual to the global. Finally, it is value-explicit and transformational (Stephenson 1989: 12; Reardon 1989: 24-25; Crews 1989: 28-37) while remaining open to a variety of values. INVST also strengthens the field of peace studies by training activist-innovators through service-learning to take its core content and values out to local communities, the nation, and other countries, where this knowledge and these values can make significant changes.

Note

1. A campus-wide Service-Learning Steering Committee created the Service-Learning Center in 1993, to serve as a locus for campus and campus-community service-learning activities. The Steering Committee subsequently created a Service-Learning Faculty Council and Service-Learning Program Council. The former includes faculty and instructors and focuses on issues of pedagogy and curriculum development. The latter serves as a venue for representatives from diverse programs to network and collaborate on activities related to service and service-learning.

References

Crews, Robin J. (1989). "A Values-Based Approach to Peace Studies." In *Peace and World Order Studies: A Curriculum Guide,* edited by D.C. Thomas and M.T. Klare, pp. 28-37. Boulder, CO: Westview Press.

Myers-Lipton, Scott J. (1994). "The Effects of Service-Learning on College Students' Attitudes Toward Civic Responsibility, International Understanding, and Racial Prejudice." Ph.D. Dissertation, Sociology Department, University of Colorado at Boulder.

Lopez, George A. (1989). "Conceptual Models for Peace Studies Programs." In *Peace and World Order Studies: A Curriculum Guide,* edited by D.C. Thomas and M.T. Klare, pp. 73-86. Boulder, CO: Westview Press.

Rank, Carol. (1989). "The Interdisciplinary Challenge of Peace Studies." In *Peace and World Order Studies: A Curriculum Guide,* edited by D.C. Thomas and M.T. Klare, p. 89. Boulder, CO: Westview Press.

Reardon, Betty. (1989). "Pedagogical Approaches to Peace Studies." In *Peace and World Order Studies: A Curriculum Guide,* edited by D.C. Thomas and M.T. Klare, pp. 24-25. Boulder, CO: Westview Press.

Stephenson, Carolyn M. (1989). "The Evolution of Peace Studies." In *Peace and World Order Studies: A Curriculum Guide,* edited by D.C. Thomas and M.T. Klare, pp. 9-19. Boulder, CO: Westview Press.

The Institute for Conflict Analysis and Resolution's Modest Experiment in Service-Learning

by Frank Blechman

George Mason University (GMU) is a relatively new public institution of the Commonwealth of Virginia, not quite 40 years old and an independent university only since 1970. Unable to compete with better established public and private universities in the state and region, GMU grew by finding unique niches, areas unfilled by the older established academic powers. GMU would cement its public support through service to the Northern Virginia community. No ivory tower, it would become the "information university," the "interactive university," a model for the 21st century. Innovation and community service would be the watchwords of the 1980s and 1990s.

Conflict Resolution at George Mason University

In 1978, discussion began at GMU about establishing an interdisciplinary peace studies or conflict resolution program. There was some thought that GMU might be able to attract national resources if it had an established program in a peace-related field. A "center" for conflict studies developed, drawing together faculty from psychology, sociology, anthropology, communication, political science, international relations, business, economics, and public policy. In 1982, the state approved a distinct master's degree, a Master of Science in Conflict Management, and the center proudly welcomed the first students to one of the first graduate degree programs in conflict resolution in the world. In 1987, a doctoral degree in conflict analysis and resolution was added. Today, the program, known as the Institute for Conflict Analysis and Resolution (ICAR), has more than 150 graduates, a core faculty of 11, with 65 active M.S. and 55 active Ph.D. students. It hosts visiting scholars, conducts research, and collaborates on intervention projects from around the world, and is well regarded as a center for the study of deeply rooted, large-scale social conflicts.

Although many students and faculty come to ICAR from peace studies and espouse values of peace, change, and justice, the ICAR curriculum is not strictly speaking a program of study in peace studies or social change or social justice. Nor is it a program in peace history. Although some historic peace processes are analyzed, much of the study involves understanding currently ongoing, evolving conflict situations. Unlike programs in history or international relations, the framing questions at ICAR are not so much, What did (historical figure X) do in this situation to cause war or peace? or How could war have been avoided or peace achieved? but rather, What could *you* do in this situation? or What resources would *you* need to effectively intervene? For some students, this focus is profoundly disappointing. It is much easier to talk about what Henry Kissinger or Kaiser Wilhelm did than to explore one's own capacities and weaknesses. Other students recognize the benefit of examining conflict without absolutely predetermining a preferred platform, approach, or outcome. Many appreciate the challenge posed by integrating theory, history, and practice with their own personality and capabilities. Most emerge vastly better equipped to analyze and transform conflicts.

The curriculum design has thus always made integration an explicit goal. Unlike programs teaching techniques for negotiation or dispute settlement, ICAR has required students to understand the sources, dynamics, processes, *and* outcomes of conflict. From the start, students, regardless of background or interests, were required to take courses in theory and practice. Required labs and internships made students wrestle with conflicts on the interpersonal, community, organizational, national, and global levels. Since most students were midcareer learners, they also brought significant personal and work experience into their studies and classes.

In 1991, the curriculum was modified to include an even larger component of fieldwork. All doctoral students were required, and master's students could elect, to spend a year (nominally a six-credit course that runs for an academic year, fall to spring) working as part of ongoing field teams organized around the following themes:

Conflicts in divided societies: Situations like South Africa or Northern Ireland in which racial, religious, or ethnic definitions of identity have separated permanently coexisting communities.

Conflicts in governance: Communities facing divisive issues in which formal and informal communication channels create solidarity or promote divisions.

Racial and ethnic conflicts in schools: Situations in which some of the same divisions and dynamics found in divided societies can be studied among adolescents, whose identities have not yet been rigidly formed, and in environments (schools) that nominally supported intergroup harmony.

Each team had multiple activities, each involving faculty and students working together with community allies or colleagues. This Applied Practice and Theory (APT) program now attracts participation by more than half of

ICAR's students, and is the unit to be examined in the remainder of this essay.

APT as Service-Learning

APT was created with several goals in mind: first, to develop, test, and integrate conflict-resolving theories and practices in communities experiencing significant conflict; second, to provide service to those communities; and third, to help students learn the value of community and community service to professional practice.

The first is the most traditional "academic" goal, albeit pursued in a practicum setting. Students initially anticipated that this would be their greatest challenge. However, the second and third goals, which are at the heart of service-learning, have actually proven far more elusive over time. "Service," by definition, is not the same thing as "practice," "research," or "experimentation." Service demands interaction between the server and the served in a relationship of mutual understanding and respect. Without this concept of service, the interaction becomes deceptive, manipulative, or worse.

First Lessons: Almost immediately, the teams discovered that tidy academic models could not be applied directly to real situations without substantial modification. For example, the divided-societies project drew on experience in international conflicts to develop models to apply in an ethnically diverse community in Washington, DC. Despite the fact that this community had experienced a decade of ethnic turbulence and several days of civil disorder in 1991 that appeared to be defined along ethnic lines, students found that they could identify as many cases of cross-cultural cooperation as of hostility. Although the media described an ethnically defined (Hispanic, Vietnamese, East African, yuppie white) and divided community, many residents did not perceive themselves or their community that way. They saw their community as a complex web of personal relationships, some of which worked well and others less well. Furthermore, different people within the "community," and even apparently within the same ethnic group, defined its boundaries and landmarks very differently. Each had his or her own concepts of the center, the main streets, and the edges. Each had unique ideas as to who and what lay within the community and outside of it, what held it together and pushed it apart. Community residents described a more complex and dynamic reality than that seen by outside observers. Accordingly, they tended to reject information or solutions brought by those with less complex or more rigid views, including ICAR.

In a similar vein, the team working on racial and ethnic conflict in schools quickly learned that it needed to study harmonious schools before it could assess conflictual ones. The members discovered that the most diverse schools were not the most conflictual, and that the most common intergroup conflicts in middle and high schools were based not on race or ethnicity but on gender!

At first sight, the governance team seemed to have a different experience. It intervened in a conflict between a community and the petroleum industry over the location, management, and operation of an aging, leaking oil tank farm. It skillfully convened discussions, facilitated joint analysis, mediated fact-finding, and constructed a civil framework for discussions of complicated issues. It helped state, federal, and private organizations work together and ensured that the voices of ordinary citizens would be heard. It was thanked by all for its service to the community. But in the end, the dispute continued to simmer in political, legislative, and legal forums, and the underlying issue (safety and acceptance or danger and relocation of the tank farm) remained substantially unresolved.

Surveys, focus groups, field interviews, and observations had produced "data." Established techniques for research and intervention had been tested, yet little new knowledge had been created. Reports of that knowledge were well received but had little impact. Could it be that our "expertise" might not be what the communities needed or wanted?

Second Lessons: We had a mantra, "We are here to serve the community," but its complexities and implications took time to sink in. The teams began with the notion that "research" and "conflict intervention" would be their major forms of community service. They imagined that the challenge would be making their advanced knowledge and skills accessible to community people not equally schooled. Students and some faculty both had to recalibrate. Their inability to easily define either *communities* or *conflicts* confounded the smooth application of models for community conflict resolution. Experienced faculty and community mentors became particularly valuable as they helped the teams slow down, reassess what they knew and needed to know, and redevelop their relationships with communities.

By the end of the first year, the meaning of the term *partnership* was maturing. It became more obvious that community-based institutions and residents had at least as much to teach as did the academics. The unspoken concept of "service to" or "service for" was becoming "service with." At this point, the hard work began.

Evolving Operating Rules: In the five years since APT began, the program has adopted a nontraditional pattern. Although students still "take" an academic "course," new students are recruited for teams in the spring of the year and are integrated into ongoing projects over the spring and summer. They catch up by reading files, meeting people, asking questions and "getting up to speed." The *APT Field Manual* serves as a text or guide and is updated from year to year. Each new team spends months developing its internal operating procedures and establishing external relationships while exploring and negotiating community projects for the following year.

The challenges to smooth teamwork are obvious. First and foremost, the teams are asymmetrical. Some team members are graduate students, who pay money and get graded. (Even among graduate students, doctoral students tend to have a greater interest in testing theory, while master's students often want to refine practice techniques.) Some are students who are working with the teams (auditing the course) but not getting graded, and so feel less obligation to do all of the background reading and fieldwork. Some are assigned faculty, while other faculty participate at a less formal level because of their interest in the projects. There are alumni and community supporters who participate because of their interest in the issues or stakes in the communities. Each brings individual knowledge and experience. Unlike the situation in a traditional course in a traditional curriculum, the team can never assume that everyone shares jargon, background, values, or goals.

Usually, the team "plan" is developed by early fall (October) and the primary "fieldwork" begins. There are still many requests for research, training, and facilitation, but team activities now are more likely to be community activities in which our faculty and students play supporting roles rather than featured ones. Team members still read, still do classic research, still debate how theories apply and how applications really work, and occasionally write papers. Yet, from October to March the flow from field experience to the classroom and back is nearly continuous. This partnership continues though the spring, when recruitment of the next team and the transition to it begins. By late spring, many teams have begun to write up their "findings" for reference or publication. Recently, however, more and more of these publications have been joint projects involving students working with others.

A Case Study: One team's struggle illuminates the challenges of service-learning in APT. In the spring of 1996, the schools team conducted very successful dialogues between gang leaders and the police. These discussions provided a valuable platform for each of the participants. Police gained information about gang youth and were able to modify their behavior to reduce unnecessary conflict. Gang leaders, reciprocally, came to understand the police better and were able to modify their behavior to avoid hassles. Students constantly applied theory to practice and vice versa as the dialogues progressed. And the community benefited with significantly lowered violence.

The 1996-97 team inherited this success story just as public attention to the issue of youth violence was peaking in the Washington, DC region. The team found that it had more offers than it could accept: invitations from other communities to replicate the previous year's success; offers to participate in conferences; opportunities to speak and teach in schools and at PTA meetings; requests to write about the dialogues for varied audiences; and appeals to expand into new and politically attractive areas.

How should the team decide which projects to pick? The faculty and previous teams provided suggestions about the pluses and minuses of various options. Each potential community partner made a compelling case why its project would provide the *best* service-learning opportunity. Individual team members had interests and relationships that pulled them toward particular possibilities and away from others. It took this team nearly three months (one-third of its course time) to sort through the possibilities and begin work.

Was this lost time wasted? From the community's viewpoint, it certainly was frustrating. But during that delay, the team and the community partners refined their mutual understanding and expectations. The resulting projects are still complex, challenging, and filled with surprises. But the result is a better partnership. Students have learned both how to do conflict resolution and how to engage in community service.

Evaluation

Students report that APT is a unique but exhausting experience. It teaches teamwork instead of competition. It teaches response to complex demands instead of the comparatively easy task of "psyching" out the professor. It treats reading and secondary research as contextual rather than authoritative material. For many doctoral students, APT has caused them to rethink their dissertation plans, both in terms of topic and methodology. It puts theory to the test.

For some students APT is the best course at ICAR, truly achieving the promised integration of theory, practice, research, and ethics. Most report that their concept of community partnerships has expanded, and many say that they intend to continue participatory forms of practice after leaving ICAR. In contrast, a few students experience APT as the most frustrating or disappointing course in the curriculum. In these cases, the conflict between academics and community life has proven unresolvable. For these students, projects did not develop on the timetable provided by an academic year. Activities produced ambiguous results. Theories were proven wrong, without time left to try again.

The same ambiguity exists among community partners. Many find the relationship with an innovative, energetic academic program beneficial; some find it less so, reporting that the annual turnover and having to get new students up to speed is annoying and significantly impedes badly needed work.

Program Design

Most academic courses are designed by instructors to provide certain predetermined experiences and to achieve preset goals. APT has evolved into an experiment in cooperative learning involving faculty, students, and communities. The objectives and activities are not and cannot be firmly preset. Faculty, admittedly, retain enormous influence on project selection, goals, standards, and team styles. Faculty try to ensure that the community work "does no harm" and take official responsibility for reporting grades to the university. But students and community members, along with faculty, define the projects, define goals, and evaluate outcomes.

This design acknowledges and responds to many of the most common challenges to good academy-community relationships.

1. **Goals.** Students and academics want to learn new things and test new ideas. Communities want tried-and-true approaches that might help them; they do not want to be guinea pigs. The APT program combines old methods with new ones and is always aware of and straightforward about the risks of trying new approaches.

2. **Timetables.** Community life ebbs and flows, but it doesn't respect academic cycles. Some community needs peak during the summer when regular academic activities have a break. Needs arise on weekends, holidays, and at night. APT is now a year-round program recognizing that it must work with the cycles of the community more than the reverse.

3. **Values and Rewards.** Graduate students want good grades and the reassurance that they are doing worthwhile academic work. Publications in specialized professional journals are a unique form of acceptance. In conflict analysis and resolution, ego (or perhaps arrogance) pushes students to delve ever deeper into more complex levels of analysis, seeking the most profound (and enticing) sources of conflict. Many communities are quite happy when the worst symptoms of conflict are relieved. Communities may not want to struggle beyond that point of initial success. APT's annual cycle actually helps academy-community relationships by strongly supporting periodic reassessment.

Furthermore, any new discipline — and conflict resolution is a comparatively new field of academic study — faces additional problems. These include the following:

4. **Theoretical Foundation.** The theories on which conflict resolution is based are not fully developed or well articulated. In contrast, a medical clinic has 3,000 years of medical knowledge and 300 years of continuous Western science to draw upon in explaining methods and approaches to a community being served. Many, if not all, of the foundational concepts of modern medicine are already popularly known and accepted, even if they

are poorly understood or followed. Conflict resolution, on the other hand, is counterintuitive, even countercultural to much in America's adversarial culture. Our jargon is still hard to translate into everyday language. Services based on such a foundation are inevitably unstable. The APT teams have worked especially hard to help communities articulate why they want to do certain things and why they think those things will be helpful. In exchange, we try to do the same, taking extra care to explain why we do what we do.

5. **Expectations.** Since many people don't quite know what conflict resolution is, they easily develop unrealistic expectations about what it can do. People reasonably expect that a university team will bring "answers" and will "fix" community or personal problems. Some may even resent our approach of working with them to help them understand and resolve their own issues. It is very easy to be pulled into roles for which we are not trained or equipped, such as social worker, therapist, counselor, or parent. APT devotes several sessions at the beginning of each project to highlighting this hazard so that all participants expect it and are better prepared to handle it. Nonetheless, this remains a problematic area.

APT as Service-Learning in Peace Studies

Is the APT program a prototype for service-learning in peace studies? Neither "conflict resolution" nor "peace studies" can claim the study of social harmony and conflict as its exclusive domain. Lawyers, social workers, therapists, religious leaders, political leaders, economists, psychologists, sociologists, anthropologists, business leaders, community developers, and dozens of others care about the same question: How do people get along?

Because our question is so broad, inevitably our efforts to integrate education and community service in a service-learning program will intersect and potentially compete with others. Our approaches will sometimes contradict and even interfere with the proposals and plans of more powerful social actors.

Do we have a unique role to play? We at ICAR believe that our service-learning program does create unique opportunities. We bring a perspective that aims to value all other views in the arena. We may disagree with others, but we do not dismiss or devalue them. Ideologically prepared and inclined to share credit, we do not have to be the only program, to declare that our approach has been the only one doing any good, or that our work is the best. We value teamwork and cooperation and bring that value into our partnerships.

Consistent with this, we will not claim that APT is a perfected model for service-learning in peace studies. We know that the program could be improved by three things. First, we need to do more to help students connect their APT experience to other courses or to subsequent work. Second, we should build simpler and more consistently applied criteria to evaluate the quality and benefits of the work done. And finally, we must work harder to articulate the learning in more diverse locations and to more varied audiences.

We can say, however, that this is one evolving model worth review. And we can report that students, faculty, and community partners alike affirm that it should remain as a featured part of the ICAR curriculum.

Peaceful Intent: Integrating Service-Learning Within a Master's in International Service at Roehampton Institute London

by Christopher Walsh and Andrew Garner

The M.A. in International Service is one of the first curricular projects of the Centre for International Service-Learning at Roehampton Institute. One of the center's aims is to stimulate international understanding and to study the contribution of service-learning to a better world order. The new M.A. fulfills this aim by placing the ideals of a peace-centered approach within an a posteriori service-learning pedagogy. Awareness of the history of service-learning and a measure of skepticism toward service-learning and peace studies within British academic circles led the course team to focus on the program's unique integration strategy as a means to secure its success. The Development Studies module provides an example of this integration and illustrates how a program can achieve a broad "peaceful" agenda together with powerful learning experiences.

This essay discusses the integration strategy for a new British master's in international service (first intake 1997) developed by Roehampton Institute London (RIL), the International Partnership for Service-Learning New York (PSL), the Autonomous University of Guadalajara Mexico (AUG), and the Kingston University of Technology Jamaica (KUT). One of the dangers of philanthropically or altruistically underpinned programs such as the M.A. in International Service is that they become victims of their own good intent, sacrificing academic rigor for misplaced community "service." On the other hand, as Kendall (1990) has pointed out, there is a general consensus "that there is something uniquely powerful about the combination of service and learning, [and] that there is something fundamentally more dynamic in the integration of the two than in either alone" (19). The program team wished to achieve the latter while guarding against the attendant risks. The comprehensive integration strategy that was developed to achieve this is discussed below and illustrated through the Development Studies and Development of Altruism and Public Service modules.

The M.A. in International Service – Course Summary

It will be helpful to look first at an overview of the program and its aims and outcomes. The program is delivered in three phases: predeparture preparation, in-country program, and the RIL program. The organization, rationale, and outcomes of each phase are summarized in "Overview of the Programme" (at the end of this essay). Initially, students receive a predeparture preparation course arranged jointly by RIL, PSL, and staff from the overseas universities. This introductory material is key in setting classroom and experiential parameters and as orientation for the overseas placement. Skills in critical observation and reflection, essential to the success of the in-country experiential learning, are established through a "preflection paper" (discussed below).

The entire in-country program, the heart of the M.A., is designed as an integrated module in service-learning that combines service in the local community with academic learning and personal growth. The module provides practical and challenging experience in a service placement attending to local development issues. This allows links to be made among the service experience, academic study of culture and history, and, through engagement and reflection, awareness of personal development. One way in which these links are achieved is through a "learning and development journal" that students are required to write. During this semester, students, with the guidance of in-country staff, also begin to formulate plans for their thesis. The thesis is unique in requiring, after conclusions and recommendations, an outline funding proposal that the in-country agency may use to attract funds. This pattern will be repeated in London as students continue to serve in local agencies and international organizations. They also take five academic modules: Research Methods in the Social Sciences; Structure and Management of Not-for-Profit Organisations; Development of Altruism and Public Service; Development Studies; and the thesis completed during the summer months.

General aims of the program include the directing of academic endeavor toward local and global problems through service-learning. The specific aims include a generic preparation of students for careers in international service, including work in development, relief, and educational organizations, in private and voluntary organizations, and in governmental agencies.

The Challenges of Service-Learning

The program team (including as many as 19 teaching staff from all four institutions) have identified two primary challenges in establishing the new M.A. program: first, in the relationship between the underlying philosophy and practical application, and second, with perceptions of service-learning within academia.

The outcomes listed above are underpinned by a philosophy that is laudable but deeply problematic. The M.A., like most service-learning programs, is built on notions of altruism, peace, and service in the community, aimed in a general sense toward a "better world order." The relationship between this underlying philosophy and the "serviced" communities deserves close attention, as past experiences in service-learning have shown. In essence, the question is: How can the "good intentions" implicit in the M.A. in International Service, built on the values of a Judeo-Christian heritage, mesh with the values and needs of the potentially "serviced" communities? Can a program like this avoid paternalism and yet still achieve its vision for a better world? How can commensurability between partners be assured?

The second challenge involves locating a service-learning master's within an equivocal academic community, many of whom consider service-learning to be lightweight, soft-headed, escapist, and not worthy of academic credit. This response is not surprising if we remember that, according to Moore (1990), a service-learning pedagogy fundamentally challenges the "traditional definitions of knowledge and the historical arrangements of power on which a university operates" (279).

The intellectual and analytical rigor enforced by the response of the academic community and by the fundamental danger of paternalism has led the program team to develop a detailed integration strategy that attempts to answer both problematics.

Overall Structural Integration Strategy

Three key elements inform the design of the program that provide structural integration: grounded experience, action research, and development of learning agendas and monitoring of personal growth.

Grounded Experience: The unifying principle of this M.A. is the pedagogical combination of experience of service, in this case in an international setting, with academic study. Many academic programs adopt, either intentionally or unintentionally, an a priori approach in which experience is secondary to the professional view of the world that is gradually unfolded to initiates. From this perspective the world is carefully crafted by practitioners through a thorough theoretical orientation, so before trainees are sent out into their placements they are immersed within this particular construction of reality. Little of the foundations and substructure of meanings is left to the grounded interpretations of initiates. Then, through professionally guided experience, the architecture of professional nuance is slowly built up in the performance repertoire of the initiate — a process, so to speak, of fitting experience into preformed theories.

Within the a priori model of training, the world is tamed to fit professional or organizational objectives, and the guiding hand of experience is no longer free to act on the learner. It may be termed correctly a "pedagogy of reification" in which teachers react to their theories as if they were part of the objective world — the real world. As Berger and Luckmann (1973) once pointed out, reification is a recognition that humankind is often incapable of remembering its own authorship of the human world. The international program team was concerned not to fall into the trap of reification, which in pedagogical terms is capable of denying the autonomy of humankind in the continuing creation and re-creation of its world, and is the antithesis of critical thinking. The team was intent upon developing a program that focused on the actual qualities of life in different parts of the globe, and for this reason it was not difficult (despite faculty resistance) to move from the traditional academic a priori approach, with its in-built tendency to reification of the world, to an a posteriori approach: in other words, allowing experience to test theories, rather than theories to form the experience — an abundantly *academic* process.

Action Research: In addition to the focused modules and the provision of service-learning experiences across the two semesters, the program is further integrated by a special thesis that has an action result in the form of an outline funding proposal. It was thought that the research element of the program should address real problems and have some result in the attraction of resources to the problem. The thesis incorporates the research methods and material usually found in an academic thesis, followed by policy recommendations and an outline funding proposal identified by the student in conjunction with her or his placement agency. This may be subsequently submitted by the agency to a funding body, ensuring a certain degree of symmetry in the service relationship. The potential for direct application and the focus on real problems identified in-country encourage active initiation, involvement, and commitment from the students. In addition, the thesis provides a point of sustained focus within the other modules across both semesters.

Development of Learning Agendas and Monitoring of Personal Growth: Throughout the program, students are required to develop and demonstrate responsibility for their own learning. In the first instance, students write an orientation, or "preflection," paper that acts as a benchmark for estimating future development. Preflection, which involves students setting out their expectations, and what they hope to achieve and learn about themselves and others, is an important strategy for enriching the whole reflective process (Falk 1995). It also crucially involves creative imagination: Students are encouraged to imagine what the agency experience will be like, and how they will react to the context and culture. The experience of critical and challenging situations encourages students to contemplate alternative images of themselves and their roles.

One important tool for tapping these insights is the "learning and development journal" in which the placement experiences are recorded and analyzed in a systematic way (the preflection paper introduces the style and parameters required). This allows the relationship among academic study, experience, and personal growth to be explored in a realistic and practical manner. It motivates students both to view the module materials as something active within their own lives and also to view their experience as dynamic within the curriculum. As Fisher (1996) observes, "the interpersonal dynamics of the journal entries foster . . . the idea of process and exchange rather than product." It also leads to a limited objectification of self that "often grants students a new and refreshing understanding of who they are and what they have experienced" in the interpersonal and social worlds (158). Finally, there is a process of personal empowerment as students become active producers of knowledge rather than passive recipients.

Integrating Service-Learning With Peace and Development Studies

The key principles of the integration strategy outlined above provide a framework for answering the challenges delineated in this section, which examines how the example of the integration of the Service-Learning module and the Development Studies module enhances the underlying "peaceful" elements. The argument made here is that these modules are two sides of the same learning experience, and that both together achieve the broad aims of a peaceful agenda in ways far more effective than would occur in a traditional, academic peace studies course.

Effective Service-Learning: The design of the Service-Learning and Development Studies modules is determined by the overall integration strategy of the program, which reflects the cyclical pattern of effective experiential learning. Gibbs and Habeshaw (1989: 34) identify four stages in the experiential cycle: experiencing, reflecting, thinking, and planning. The program starts with predeparture preparation (the planning stage), which involves orientation and preflection, and moves to the in-country active learning experience. It is through the modules run at Roehampton that more time is given to the "thinking" elements of the cycle — interpreting and making sense of the data, defining and acknowledging parameters, generalizing, and developing hypotheses and principles. Finally, through the thesis and funding proposal, students actively prepare and plan for the next experience.

Various organizational and pedagogical tools reinforce this effective learning. Organizationally, students are placed in agencies that have a long relationship with the local university and subsequently with PSL (e.g., AUG was founded on the principle of service and is a major provider of health services to the poor in the city). The service is jointly monitored by experienced members of the in-country teaching teams and specified agency staff. Later, students' work is assessed by an international program team.

The teaching and learning methods employed in both modules emphasize participation that makes pedagogical use of the students' experiences in the agency and in the wider society. In addition, both formative and summative assessment require students to draw explicitly on the taught elements, group and tutorial discussion, reading assignments, and agency experience (see "General Programme Assessment Categories" at the end of this essay). The last of these is available in fieldwork form in the "learning and development journal" that students write and discuss with tutors on a regular basis across all phases of the program.

The Development Studies module fulfills the requirements of an effective learning cycle by providing guided reflection on the in-country experiences. It supplies a framework for exploring and developing higher cognitive skills within an established academic field (thus, in part, answering faculty reservations about academic standing). Development Studies is, after all, the academic arena for understanding the *causes* of many of the *effects* students will observe during their in-country placement. It is in this understanding that we believe the program's underpinning "peaceful" aims are achieved.

Teaching "Peace": In their book on societies at peace, anthropologists Howell and Willis (1989) argue that "violent and peaceful social interaction is not to be understood through the search for a thing called 'aggression,' but through the sensitive and detailed explication of values and meanings that embody and shape behaviour in different social settings" (22). This is predicated on the idea that humans are a priori social beings and that their actions only make sense embedded in shared sets of meanings (2-7). Thus, part of achieving the program's "peaceful" agenda involves direct personal engagement with different sets of meanings through the service-learning experience. To put it another way: War is understood not only by an examination of peace negotiations but also through studying the sets of meanings that make conflict possible. Therefore, the main purpose of the Development Studies module is to understand the sociocultural, economic, and political exchanges of a global environment that form the conditions students experience overseas.

Linking Critical Thinking and Experiential Reflection: The module aims to foster a deep approach (Biggs and Collis 1982; Biggs 1987, 1990) to learning by building on the motivational context of the program, which encourages personal reflection on experience; nourishing an independent learning environment in which personal growth and problem-based learning are linked; and establishing group work and interaction with others as an effective arena for sharing reflections and evaluating data. Linking this approach to a well-structured knowledge base allows students space to develop their critical and evaluative skills. The program team has thus put great store in encouraging the formation of "the habit of examining ideas for their logical soundness and empirical support" (Logan 1976: 30, *cf* Weast 1996). A careful observation and recording of the multiplicities of agency activities within policy and delivery fields, and subsequent reflection on them, bring a rich store of empirical activity to the London-based modules. This dynamic incorporation of critical thinking and experiential reflection is illustrated in the organization, syllabus, and delivery of the Development Studies module (see "Development Studies Module: Organisation and Syllabus" at the end of this essay).

Personal Growth and Development Studies: Another dynamic incorporation in the program is that between micro personal development and macro social and economic development. The related motifs of development, change, and growth are pedagogically addressed within the module. This approach recognizes an intuitive link between personal and social change reflected in the colloquialism that "you cannot expect to change others until you first attend to changing yourself." But pedagogically, the approach also recognizes the transferability of insights about the dynamics of personal growth and integration to social change and peace.

Altruism Studies: The "peaceful" elements within the Development Studies module are also reinforced by "peaceful" elements within the Development of Altruism module. This module addresses one of the central questions posed by traditional courses in ethics and welfare: How do we move from intellectual analysis of ethical and altruistic issues to a betterment of others and self-growth? This is a question clearly posed by Robert Coles: "How does one move from an intellectual analysis of ethical issues to a life that is honorable and decent?" (1990: 2). The course aims to provide students with a thorough understanding of altruistic service-learning and its relationship to voluntarism, philanthropy, the development of human welfare in political contexts, and social education and personal development. The aim of preparing students for careers in international agencies that are concerned with improving the quality of life for people is enhanced by linking intellectual analysis with the students' experiences of working in the agencies. (See "Development of Altruistic Service Module: Syllabus" at the end of this essay.)

Conclusion

It was indeed fortunate for the program that an undergraduate international network already existed, but nevertheless, it still remains a challenge to plan and deliver an integrated, experiential master's course across four countries with very different languages and cultures. The practicalities of organizing this, of communicating effectively and ensuring mutuality, are simply a microcosm of efforts to avoid the dangers of paternalism in the program as a whole. The careful integration strategy adopted is founded on an explicit recognition that service-learning as we imagine it is embedded in Western notions of altruism. Rather than throwing out the "baby" of a powerful learning with the "bathwater" of implicit good intentions, the team has adopted an integration strategy that explicitly builds on an a posteriori approach that allows experience and direct engagement to be the guiding hand in individual and social change. Through this integration the challenge of locating a service-learning master's within a traditional academic community is achieved without sacrificing established pedagogies. Such an integration strategy takes the notion of a posteriori learning to heart by ensuring that personal engagement with different meaning systems is the essential first base in understanding, and understanding is itself a major step in achieving peaceful aims.

References

Berger, P., and T. Luckmann. (1973). *The Social Construction of Reality: A Treatise in the Sociology of Knowledge*. Harmondsworth, Middlesex: Penguin.

Biggs, J.B. (1987). *Student Approaches to Studying and Learning*. Melbourne: Australian Council for Educational Research.

——— . (1990). "Teaching Design for Learning." Keynote paper, Higher Education Research and Development Society of Australia meeting, Brisbane.

——— , and K.F. Collis. (1982). *Evaluating the Quality of Learning: The SOLO Taxonomy*. New York, NY: Academic Press.

Coles, R. (Fall 1990). "Action/Reflection." Newsletter. New York, NY: Partnership for Service-Learning.

Falk, D. (1995). "Preflection: A Strategy for Enhancing Reflection." *NSEE Quarterly* 21(2): 13.

Fisher, B.J. (1996). "Using Journals in the Social Psychology Class: Helping Students Apply Course Concepts to Life Experiences." *Teaching Sociology* 24: 157-165.

Gibbs, G., and T. Habeshaw. (1989). *Preparing to Teach: An Introduction to Effective Teaching in Higher Education*. Bristol, Avon: Technical and Educational Services Ltd.

Howell, S., and R. Willis. (1989). *Societies at Peace: Anthropological Perspectives*. London: Routledge.

Kendall, J.C., and Associates, eds. (1990). *Combining Service and Learning: A Resource Book for Community and Public Service, Volume 1*. Raleigh, NC: National Society for Experiential Education.

Logan, C. (1976). "Do Sociologists Teach Students to Think More Critically?" *Teaching Sociology* 4: 29-48.

Moore, D. (1990). "Experiential Education as Critical Discourse." In *Combining Service and Learning: A Resource Book for Community and Public Service, Volume 1,* edited by J.C. Kendall and Associates. Raleigh, NC: National Society for Experiential Education.

Roehampton Institute London. (1996). MA *International Service Outline Programme Proposal.*

Weast, D. (1996). "Alternative Teaching Strategies: The Case for Critical Thinking." *Teaching Sociology* 24: 189-194.

Overview of the Programme

	July/August Pre-departure Preparation	September/December In-country programme	February/June Roehampton Institute, London programme	End of August
Course organisation	Prepared jointly by RIL, PSL & overseas university. Introduction to the course, placement, and distance learning quality. 'Preflection paper'.	International Service-Learning module. This consists of : Placement in a local agency and three integrated courses at partner institutions: • Social Structure and Cultural Studies • Contemporary Social Policy Issues • Language and Literature Studies 'Learning & Development Journal'.	• Placement in local agency Five Academic Modules; • Research Methods in the Social Sciences • Structure and Management of Not-For-Profit Organisations • Development of Altruism and Public Service • Development Studies • Thesis and Outline Funding Proposal	Hand in Thesis with outline funding proposal
Course Rationale	Setting academic and experiential parameters of Service Learning MA; establishing individual expectations and requirements; orientation for placement.	Integration of service in local community with academic learning and personal growth. Direct experiential learning through immersion in the society, culture and working environments in a development setting. Develop a student and problem centred approach through specific examples and reflexive observation and writing.	These courses build on *a posteriori* experiential model, subjecting personal experience to academic analysis and rigour in an active learning environment. They develop the student and problem centred approach on two levels; on a practical dimension (research methods, writing and presentation skills, organisational structures) and on a theoretical dimension (applying traditional academic theoretical models to problems arising out of the experiential placements)	A bringing together of 'traditional' academic skills with the notion of service to the community (in the form of a funding application
Course Outcomes	Students are able to make effective use of their placement experience without significant 'lag-time'. i.e. they start recording, observing and reflecting critically right from the start.	Immersion in a development setting where both the routine and unpredictable complexities of social problems at a local level are experienced. Gaining competency and professionalism in working for an agency. Effective use of self reflection as an individual development tool and as a method of approaching grounded problems. To demonstrate a grasp of the social, cultural and working environments of their placement.	To demonstrate the ability to apply academic models and insights to problems that have arisen from the experiences of the previous semester. To demonstrate the ability to plan, write, and present materials on a practical problem with a sound academic understanding of the theoretical and organisational issues involved. To have set and achieved targets for personal growth.	To demonstrate the ability to write a sustained, theoretically informed thesis that deals with a practical experience - based problem and includes at the end an outline funding proposal.

General Programme

Assessment Categories

A Judgement will be made of:

1. the quality of Programme concept comprehension and grounded issues:
   students will be expected to demonstrate a strong grasp of concepts and apply them with considerable competence and insight to issues and grounded problems in their cultural and global contexts.

2. the quality of critical thinking and analysis:
   students will be expected to demonstrate an advanced capacity for critical thinking characterised by clarity of thought, logical and coherent argument, analysis of the grounded problems that confront them, critical evaluation and recommendations.

3. the quality of the critical review of current literature:
   students will be expected to have familiarised themselves thoroughly with an appropriate range of the current literature involved in their modules and to demonstrate a sophisticated and firm grasp of literature and research which they use for course assignments and in the dissertation.

4. the degree of integration of theory and experience:
   in line with the *a posteriori*, heuristic approach of the course students will be expected to demonstrate a continuous attention to the relating of experience and theory, and in their written assignments and discussion demonstrate that powerful links are being made between them. In their Learning and Development Journals they will explore these relationships in a formative way.

5. the selection and development of an appropriate methodological approach for the dissertation:
   students will be expected to provide a well justified case for the selection of methodology and to competently develop and operationalise the chosen approach. This is considered in the Research Methods modules.

6. the quality of imagination and originality of approach:
   students will be expected to demonstrate within an autonomous context a degree of imagination and creativity, beyond what is normally expected in undergraduate programmes.

7. problem solving:
   students will be expected to demonstrate a committed workmanlike approach to the solution of actual community problems.

8. the level of responsibility:

students will be expected, within the bounds of voluntary activity and practice, to demonstrate a high level of responsibility for their work within the agencies and for developing their own academic, practical and personal learning agendas (these items will be recorded on a proposed achievement profile).

9. ethical understanding:

students will be expected to be aware of ethical issues in Social Action research i.e. the relationship between the researcher and the researched. This issue is considered in the Research Methods: Qualitative Methods Module.

10. the ability to access information:

students will be expected to demonstrate in their assignments and discussion an advanced ability to effectively access selected sources of information on world problems (this item will be recorded in a proposed achievement profile).

11. the ability to disseminate and communicate:

students will be expected to demonstrate a developed capacity for communicating what they learn and for effectively working together in group situations (these items will be summatively managed in the tutor and peer assessment elements of specific modules and will also be recorded in an achievement profile).

Development Studies Module

Organisation & Syllabus

The Development Studies module is divided into two sections. The first section (weeks 1-5) places the module within the context of the overall programme, introduces definitions of development, and addresses major theories in the sociology of development. The second section (weeks 6-12) focuses on current substantive issues in development studies.

The first two sessions of section one reinforce the integrated nature of the whole programme, emphasising the particular links of the experience with the module and the dissertations. It reviews the relevant overall programme outcomes and links these to the structure and outcomes of the module. A reflective 'raising questions' session identifies expectations, alerts students to pertinent issues arising out of their in-country placement, and initiates an effective group learning environment. The framework for a well structured knowledge base is implemented by discussing definitions and measures of development, and introducing the evolution of key classical and contemporary theories. These will then be placed within two major theoretical perspectives: modernisation theories and conflict theories. In the following sessions students will present a summary and discussion of a theorist or perspective selected from a prepared list with appropriate readings.

Section two allows students to share in the planning and structure of their own learning in the Development Studies module - thus providing a framework for deep learning practices and critical reflection. Making use of their Learning and Development Journal, and considering theoretical issues raised by section one of the module, students identify a grounded critical issue (which reflects students' on-going planning for the dissertation element). Tutors guide students towards current substantive development issues in the light of the student's specific identified problem. Students then organise a timetable to present an analysis of the substantive issue, relating it to the experiential elements of the programme. Tutors will follow up with lectures appropriate to the agreed timetable. In order for this to work properly, the course team have identified and prepared reading lists for a wider range of current development issues than is actually possible to teach. These include: Global Economy and Debt; Agencies, Aid and Economic Development; Culture and Development; Colonialism and Post-Colonialism; Tourism and Development; Political Development; Social Inequality, Stratification and Development; Hunger, Disease and Development; Refugees and War; Gender and Development; Population and Urbanisation, Environment and sustainable development.

Development of Altruistic Service Module

Syllabus

1. Definitions and Competing Approaches
    Altruism
    Social and Natural Science approaches
    Altruism & voluntarism - Golding's barbarism v. Dickson's gentled society
    Service-Learning as pathway to knowledge
2. Service as experiential education
    Dewey's theory of experience - Service-Learning and the liberal arts
    Schon's reflective practitioner
    Polany's epistemology
    Critical discourse and experiential education
3. Service-learning and social responsibility
    Civic education and the liberal tradition
    Exposure v. engagement
    Personal development v social justice
4. Welfare, atruism and society
    Christian approaches to welfare
    Rise of humanitarianism & philanthropy
    The Voluntary Tradition
    Development of British state welfare in 19 & 20 centuries
    Alternative welfare systems
5. Altruism and political philosophy
    Democratic Socialism
    New Right
    Pluralism & the Middle Way
    Marxism
    Feminism
    Greenism
    Disengagement of altruism & politics
6. Crosscultural service-learning
    Intercultural literacy and intercultural capital
    Challenges to Service
7. Altruism and international aid
    The aid business
    Aid v. Help
    Critical responses

Learning About Peace Through Service:
Introduction to Peace and Conflict Studies at the University of Colorado at Boulder

by Robin J. Crews

A Brief History of Peace Studies at CU-Boulder

In 1972, the undergraduate Conflict and Peace Studies program began at the University of Colorado at Boulder. For roughly 20 years, the program took the form of an "individually structured major" within the College of Arts and Sciences. During that period of time, student and faculty interest in the program (and in the interdisciplinary field of peace studies) varied considerably.

By 1992, the curriculum had evolved into a mixed collection of seven courses: Nuclear War: Its Risks and Preventions; Ideology, Conflict and Peace; Environmental Dimensions of International Security; Topics in Peace and Conflict Studies; and three Independent Study courses at the sophomore, junior, and senior levels, all of which were offered within the program on an irregular basis. This curriculum was supplemented by a much larger group of cross-listed courses from a variety of departments that the faculty advisory committee had approved over the years as relevant to the field of peace studies. Up until that time, there were no required courses, i.e., any continuity for the major (owing in part, I imagine, to the fact that the majors were "individually structured" by the students).

In the spring of 1992, the Conflict and Peace Studies program was transformed from an "individually structured major" into a "certificate" program that allowed students to pursue their interests in peace studies in conjunction with more traditional majors at the university. This change also opened up the possibility for more students to pursue peace studies, as it did not require those interested in the field to major in it. At that time, a formal curriculum (including an introductory course and a capstone seminar) was created. Funding for the program continues to be limited to support for the two courses required for the certificate (Introduction to Peace and Conflict Studies in the fall semester and Senior Seminar in Peace and Conflict Studies in the spring).

At the time that the individually structured major was transformed into a certificate program, the name of the program was deliberately changed from Conflict and Peace Studies to Peace and Conflict Studies (PACS). As far as I could tell, it had been the only peace (and conflict) studies program left in the country whose name still began with "Conflict" instead of "Peace." This name change also reflected an intentional move away from past emphases on what I have elsewhere called "shadows of peace" to "essential peace" (Crews 1999).

Requirements for the Peace and Conflict Studies Certificate

Students are required to complete 24 hours for the certificate: two core courses and six cross-listed courses. Given the interdisciplinary nature of peace studies (and the predisposition of many faculty to think and teach within their own disciplines), three of the six cross-listed courses must be within a student's major and three outside of it. This provides students with an opportunity to view the field of peace studies from both disciplinary and interdisciplinary perspectives. It also allows them to explore their own interests in peace studies as an extension of their major interests.

At present, some 110 courses in 24 departments, a residential academic program, and the International and National Voluntary Service Training Program (see the essay by Scarritt and Lowe in Part II) are included on the list of approved courses for the PACS certificate. The remainder of this essay focuses on Introduction to Peace and Conflict Studies and explores the ways in which service-learning is integrated into the course. To highlight options and variations in service-learning requirements, I refer on occasion to a second PACS course, Nonviolence and the Ethics of Social Action, which I taught as a service-learning course in 1995 and 1996.

Introduction to Peace and Conflict Studies

This lower-division course is intended to provide students with an overview of the field, its relationship with other academic disciplines, and careers in the field. It is designed for all students interested in the fundamental issues of peace, justice, and conflict resolution in their lives, as well as for those students interested in the Peace and Conflict Studies certificate. It is taught as an interactive seminar with an enrollment limit of 25 students.

Course objectives include familiarity with the causes, symptoms, and dynamics of conflict and violence (interpersonal to global); the philosophical and theological bases of peacemaking; the causes, symptoms, and dynamics of peace (interpersonal to global); justice; human rights; non-principled and principled nonviolence; peacemaking and conflict resolution (interpersonal and macro level); activism; peace movements; women and peace; and careers in conflict resolution and peacemaking. Objectives also include learning critical-thinking skills.

As a result of the substantive shift away from "shadows of peace" topics, this course includes little on the Cold War (with the exception of an in-depth look at the decision to drop the first atomic bombs on Hiroshima and Nagasaki and the costs and consequences of this decision). To be sure, the first part of the course does examine origins of conflict, violence, and war, as part of an essential introduction to the analysis of conflict. Given my own interest in the relationships between ideology, violence, nonviolence, and peace, however, this part of the course could be seen as contributing to an understanding of the development of peace as much as it is also an analysis of the causes, symptoms, and consequences of violence.

Service-Learning Components of the Course: Introduction to Peace and Conflict Studies became a service-learning course in fall 1995. Even though I was still fairly new to service-learning at the time, I could not imagine a field of study that lent itself better to service-learning than did peace studies, i.e., given its ultimate goals of social transformation, justice, and improving the human condition. (This is treated more fully in my introductory essay in Part I of this book.)

Students are informed in the syllabus and on the first day of classes that the course involves service-learning. (Ultimately we hope to have all service-learning courses on campus identified with "SL" designations in the course catalog and schedule of courses, but at present this information is not available until the first class meeting.) Service-learning is introduced in the syllabus as follows:

> This course is designed as a "service-learning" course. Essentially this means that you will have the opportunity to augment your "traditional" learning experience in the classroom with experiential learning in the form of some kind of community service related to peace and/or conflict. Thus, you will learn about peace and conflict via service and experience — as well as through our readings and classroom discussions. We will discuss service-learning extensively at the beginning of the semester so that everyone knows what it means and understands how this aspect of the course will work.

> You will be required to (1) find an appropriate placement in a community agency (I will help you here, of course); (2) engage in three hours of service each week (for at least twelve of the fifteen weeks during the semester) which helps you explore peace and conflict in direct ways; (3) keep a journal of your experiences and learning process; and (4) write a final paper that integrates your readings and class discussions, your understanding of peace and/or conflict, and your semester's community service work. Clearly, you will need to have a great deal of self-discipline to complete this aspect of the course successfully.

In my Nonviolence course, the journal requirement for the service-learning students has evolved into five "service-learning reflections," which students must turn in on specified dates throughout the semester. For the "traditional track" students (discussed below), the journal requirement has become five "reading question sets" throughout the semester. These variations were suggested by students in previous courses who found that they lacked the self-discipline necessary for keeping a journal on their own throughout the semester and asked for additional structure and deadlines.

Service-Learning as an Option: To date, I have not required students to engage in service-learning in any of my courses: it is a choice students make for themselves. For the past few years, the debate (on the Service-Learning Discussion Group on the Internet) over whether to require service-learning in the curriculum has highlighted the strengths and weaknesses of optional vs. required service-learning courses. It is a debate that most probably will continue for years to come. [See the Appendix for more on this Web resource.]

At present, there are two compelling reasons why service-learning is optional in my courses. First, while service is *part* of the "homework" (rather than something added on top of existing homework in an otherwise "traditional" course), service-learning is a commitment that requires sufficient time outside the classroom. Thus, one concern is related to the fact that students come from a variety of socioeconomic backgrounds; those who are not on scholarship and do not receive support from their parents (in particular, nontraditional students) may need all their free time to earn rent, tuition, student fees, and book money.

Similarly, some students may be enrolled in more than one service-learning course during the same semester. Unless the same service is allowed to count toward both or all courses, it may or may not be physically possible for these students to engage in yet another course that requires service as part of the learning process. Clearly, teachers requiring service-learning need to be sensitive to additional demands on students' lives that go beyond the class in question.

Second, it has been my experience that when students consciously choose service-learning, its potential to transform their learning and their lives is increased. Although not scientifically verified (since I have never required service-learning, it is not possible for me to make a formal comparison), this observation is empirically based: It comes from student feedback through conversations, structured reflection, and faculty course questionnaires that students complete at the end of the semester.

Ironically, at the end of the semester, most students in the class agree that (1) they are glad that service-learning was not forced on them, i.e., that they were allowed to choose and that students in future classes should have the same freedom to choose; and, at the same time, (2) the service-learning aspects of the course were so important, personal, and transformative that, in their opinion, all students should somehow "do" the service-learning in the future.

In any event, for the foreseeable future, students in the course will be able to choose between service-learning and a "traditional" track. Thus, the syllabus includes the following alternative:

> If you wish, you may "opt out" of the service-learning aspects of the class. If you prefer the "traditional" track, you will be required to complete all readings, keep a journal that, in part, responds to 5-6 sets of reading questions, and complete the mid-semester take-home essays and the final take-home essays.

How Grades Differ for Service-Learning and Traditional Track Students: Whether students elect to engage in the service-learning aspects of the course or the "traditional" track, everyone must complete all the readings, attend all classes, and participate actively in class discussions (attendance is noted, but not "graded"; instead, it is used as a "fudge factor" in determining grades). I should also note that, although service-learning students must successfully complete their service in order to complete other aspects of the course, *they receive grades based on their learning and performance, not on their service.* (Additional information from the syllabus about how grades are determined for the two tracks in the Nonviolence course is reproduced at the end of this essay.)

Finding a Service-Learning Placement: Students must choose which track they wish to be in by the end of the second week of class. Those choosing service-learning must have a service-learning placement arranged and a service-learning contract signed by the end of the third week. It has been my experience that fairly firm deadlines are necessary, as many students (especially shy ones) may hesitate indefinitely in searching for off-campus service sites.

The staff at our campus's former Service-Learning Center (1993 to mid-1997) developed a list of nonprofit human service agencies in the Boulder Valley. At the beginning of each academic year, these agencies were contacted, informed about the center and service-learning, and then asked whether they wished to be included on our list of service-learning sites. This list was disseminated to all faculty interested in service-learning, with the hope that they would select specific agencies from the list that were appropriate for their service-learning courses.

This process was set up to avoid several mistakes common in service-learning at the time: (1) failure to inform community partners about service-learning activities on campus; (2) failure to invite community partners to participate in campus service-learning efforts and ask for their permission to include them in our list of potential service-learning sites; and (3) having faculty send unwanted students to these agencies without prior contact or permission. Each semester I would select from this list agencies relevant to the learning outcomes of my course. In addition, students were invited to propose additional venues for service-learning that were not included on the list.

Unfortunately, funding for our Service-Learning Center was eliminated in June 1997 as part of campus-wide budget cuts. However, during the past year, Boulder Community Network developed a virtual database of all non-profit human service agencies in Boulder County. This database (Boulder County LINC), which includes approximately 185 agencies at present, provides users (in our case, faculty, students, and staff) with updated information on each agency and the kind of service involved. I now use this virtual database as my primary means of service venue selection.

Structured Time for Service-Learning in Class: On the first day of the semester, students are introduced to service-learning as part of an overview of the course. At the end of the third week, we devote an entire class to an exploration of "service as one path to peace and justice." Here we explore in greater detail service and service-learning and their relationship to issues of peace, justice, and conflict. We also focus on service placements, contracts, and structured opportunities for reflection during the rest of the semester. Ideally, students should have their service-learning placements confirmed and their contracts signed by site supervisors by this date. Finally, this class provides an opportunity for students to share their initial impressions of service, service-learning, and their placements; i.e., it is the beginning of informal reflection through class discussion.

The last time I taught this course, I set aside only one additional class period for "structured reflection." It was still my hope at that time that students would be able to integrate what they were learning through their service into our regular class discussions without my setting aside specific classes for this purpose and nothing else. Although it may be possible to achieve this in some classes with some students, this was not possible here. One class devoted to structured reflection proved to be insufficient. Service-learning students need ample time to bring what they are learning through their service back into the classroom and engage in the sometimes difficult task of connecting their thoughts, impressions, feelings, and analyses with other aspects of the course. Furthermore, students in both tracks benefit from this process. Everyone becomes involved in reflecting on the course themes, critical questions, and different approaches to learning about them.

Therefore, in my Nonviolence course the following semester (spring 1996), the service-learning aspects of the course received much greater attention. Service-learning was again introduced on the first day of class, but students had to decide which track to take by the end of the first week of class, and the goal was to have placements and signed contracts by the end of the second week. At the end of the third week, we again devoted an entire class to an exploration of "service as one path to peace and justice." Then, rather than one class for structured reflection, there were five. This meant that one-sixth of the semester was formally devoted to service-learning classes.

Modes of Structured Reflection: This essential component of service-learning comes in many forms (see Eyler, Giles, and Schmiede 1996; Jacoby and Associates 1996). I have relied primarily on journals, "service-learning reflections" at regular intervals (brief, informal essays — not unlike journal entries), oral presentations by students, class discussions, and a final integrative paper. In the presentations and discussions, my role is to serve as a facilitator as well as to pose challenging questions that invite students to engage in critical reflection about their service and its relationship to the subject matter of the course. Similarly, students are encouraged to ask critical questions of one another and to compare service experiences, problems, and positive outcomes.

Learning Outcomes: It is difficult for me now to imagine how I taught this course in the past without service-learning. As the course is currently structured, students learn firsthand about structural violence by serving in any number of human services agencies, including homeless shelters, battered women shelters, rape and gender education programs, Native American rights groups, and community food-share programs. They learn about peacemaking, nonviolence, interpersonal conflict resolution, learned conflict styles, and parenting as they tutor, mentor, teach, and assist in preschools, family learning centers, elementary schools, junior and senior high schools, the YMCA, victim offender reconciliation programs, mediation services, Big Brothers and Big Sisters programs, and peace centers. They learn about environmental conflict by serving in city/county parks, recreation, and open-space agencies, in energy conservation groups, and in the Sierra Club, Humane Society, Green Corps, and Habitat for Humanity.

Of course, these impressions come from a teacher's perspective. What ultimately matters most is what the students take away from the class at the end of the semester. In describing "the most effective aspects of this course" in their course evaluations, various students wrote:

Being able to use our knowledge in everyday life by doing service-learning.

Service-learning is an excellent tool, especially for a . . . course involving social action.

All of the readings we did and our service-learning really brought together the ideas behind nonviolence. After a short period in this course, I found myself really being able to incorporate the ideas into my own life.

The course really promoted thought outside of class. The service-learning was a big commitment, but a worthwhile experience.

The Service-Learning Project. It really brought the class readings and discussions home.

Conclusions

Every course is an experiment for me. Like many instructors, each time I teach a course, I experiment with readings, subject matter, requirements, course outline, discussion format, grading, and the like. I took some deep breaths a few years ago to try on service-learning to see if it fit me, my preferred teaching style, peace studies, the students, and the community. It was not without some anxiety, some stumbling, some doubt, some less-than-smooth articulations of what I wanted from the students during class conversations about service-learning and some less-than-perfect, end-of-the-semester course evaluations. At first.

But as I continue to experiment with service-learning on my own, as well as learn from other faculty around me who empower their students and me with their courage and creativity, I delight in the good fortune that introduced me to service-learning. There is still much I can learn and improve upon (e.g., working more closely with community partners, helping students unpack the learning they engage in through their service, assisting the few who develop problems in selecting appropriate service-learning venues or in making the service as meaningful as possible). But I know from my students and my own inner voice that the fit — between me and service-learning and between service-learning and peace studies — is a very, very good one. I am overjoyed to have this innovative, exciting pedagogy as part of my teaching repertoire. But what pleases me even more is that service-learning has transformed "my" repertoire into "our" repertoire.

References

Crews, Robin. (1999). "Peace." In *The Oxford Companion to American Military History*, edited by John Whiteclay Chambers II. New York, NY: Oxford University Press.

Eyler, Janet, Dwight E. Giles, Jr., and Angela Schmiede. (1996). *A Practitioner's Guide to Reflection in Service-Learning: Student Voices & Reflections*. Nashville, TN: Vanderbilt University.

Jacoby, Barbara, and Associates, eds. (1996). *Service-Learning in Higher Education: Concepts and Practices*. San Francisco, CA: Jossey-Bass.

The Service-Learning Track

% of Total Grade

1. Attend all classes and participate actively in class discussions   30%

2. Complete all readings and *five* "service-learning reflections"   (20%)
   throughout the semester on specified dates.
   (included in the 50% of total grade in #3, below)

3. Find an appropriate placement in a community agency;   50%
   engage in three hours of service each week (for at least *twelve* of
   the *fifteen* weeks during the semester) which helps you explore
   nonviolence and social change in direct ways; and actively
   participate in "structured reflection" sessions about your service
   during classtime.

4. Using your "service-learning reflections" as a starting point, write   20%
   a final *integrative* paper that integrates your semester's service with
   the readings, class discussions, and your understanding of nonviolence.

The "Traditional" Track

% of Total Grade

1. Attend all classes and participate actively in class discussions   30%

2. Complete all readings and *five* reading question sets   20%
   (Each set has two questions: short essay format)

3. Complete the mid-semester take-home essays   20%

4. Complete the semester-end take-home essays   30%

Learning About Peace: Five Ways Service-Learning Can Strengthen the Curriculum

by Martha C. Merrill

Why use service-learning in a peace studies course? When I taught the introductory peace studies class at Radford University in 1995, I had five reasons for including service-learning as an option: first, to provide a unifying touchstone for the course; second, to accommodate those students whose orientation was toward activism rather than research; third, to help students understand and avoid the easy stereotyping of others that can lead to depersonalization; fourth, to involve students, in a limited sense, in crossing cultures; and fifth, to help students understand how they and others form identities, and the role such identities have in conflict. Each of these reasons will be explored in more depth below, but first, as background, I will describe the university, its students, and the course.

Background

Radford University is a comprehensive state university of 9,000 students, located in southwestern Virginia, closer to West Virginia and North Carolina than to Washington, both geographically and culturally. Many of its students come from the region, which is considered part of Appalachia. Fraternities and sororities are an important part of life for many students, and religious organizations are common. Academically, programs in health fields, education, the arts, and human services have been drawing cards for students.

The Peace and World Security Studies Program at Radford was initiated in the spring of 1993 by a group of faculty from a variety of disciplines and not without negative reaction from more conservative forces on campus. The program offers a minor, not a major, and includes a 200-level introductory course and a 400-level capstone course. Students selecting the minor choose a total of 18 semester-hour credits; the applicable courses can vary widely, depending upon the student's major and interests. The courses simply need to be approved by the coordinator of the peace studies minor, who is a volunteer without release time. He or she also coordinates the introductory course, almost invariably as an overload. The word "coordinates" rather than "teaches" is appropriate, as the course traditionally has included guest speakers from a variety of disciplines ranging from biology to religion. The course has no prerequisites and attracts students from first year through seniors and from a range of majors, including those minoring in peace studies and those who just thought the course "sounded interesting." The semester I coordinated the class, 15 students were enrolled.

Selecting the sites for student service-learning is made easier because Radford has an office, staffed with a professional and an AmeriCorps volunteer, devoted to service-learning. As coordinator of the introductory course, I did not have to find the sites and contact directors of volunteers; the director of service-learning did that for me. I told her what I wanted to accomplish with service-learning, how much time students were to spend on it, how it would be integrated into the course, and mundane details such as which students had cars. She came up with a number of sites, and we eventually selected a nursing home, a soup kitchen, a battered women's shelter (a student already was volunteering there and requested to turn her service into service-learning — with good results), and a homeless shelter, for which two Media Studies students designed publicity and fundraising materials.

Evaluation of students' performance was based on their attainment of 11 course goals (see the syllabus at the end of this essay). Students were offered the opportunity to design individualized learning contracts if they had different or additional goals, but none chose this option, possibly because the course offered a variety of other instructional techniques new to most students: email discussion groups, cohort groups, collaborative learning, and handing in weekly reading summaries in advance of class. These techniques meant that class time, other than in the case of some of the guest teachers, could be spent on discussion and on reaction to the readings, the service, and the students' research, rather than on initial contact with the material — what Barbara Walvoord (1994) calls "teaching as if the students were present." Service-learning also was new to most of the students, although service itself was not. Whether or not the goals were attained was evaluated not only by myself, as instructor, but also by the students themselves individually and, to a lesser extent, by students in a group, as members of a cohort group evaluated their group's efforts. The class was divided into two cohort groups, a service-learning group and a research group (see the syllabus), for reasons that will be discussed below. Student grades were based on demonstration of course goals through performance in a variety of activities, to accommodate various student strengths and learning styles.

Reasons for Incorporating Service-Learning

The pedagogy of service-learning assisted students in meeting the course goals in five ways, some pragmatic and some more conceptual. First, on the more pragmatic side, involvement in service-learning or on research projects and the use of cohort groups related to them provided a way of unifying a course that could seem fragmented owing to the number of guest speakers involved. It should be mentioned, too, that a "guest speaker" is not necessarily a "guest lecturer," but rather a "guest teacher," most of whom used teaching methodologies focused on student involvement, and several of whom attended the class regularly. The guest teachers' methods included a spirited debate between two ecologists, some probing questioning after slides depicting animal aggression, give-and-take with refugee families, and so forth. As mentioned, the "instructor of record" traditionally has served as the course coordinator more than as the course teacher. This has been true for two reasons: First, the faculty involved are scholars in a variety of fields, and none has a degree in peace studies per se, so no one person has the interdisciplinary expertise to speak to all aspects of peace studies. Second, except for the semester when I taught the course, it has been assigned to faculty only as an overload, thereby allowing for limited preparation time.

This reliance on guest teachers, although a positive learning tool in the breadth of approaches to which students are exposed, can also make the course seem fragmented to students who are not equipped to provide their own structure for the course. The cohort groups, one for the service-learners and one for the researchers, and the idea of an ongoing project, either in service-learning or in research, were designed to bring coherence into the course and to allow the students to see the various pieces as part of a whole, as a series of different lenses with which to examine service or research and the concept of peace itself.

A second reason for using service-learning in the course was to recognize the divide sometimes seen in the peace studies literature: that between activists and researchers. Approximately half of the students in the class did service, kept journals, and composed an ongoing paper called "Profile of an Agency," an assignment adapted from curricula developed by the International Partnership for Service-Learning. The other half chose a particular country or conflict and examined how the issues raised in class related to that country or conflict. In choosing whether to participate in the service-learning or the research track, students had to engage in reflection about why they were taking the course and what their interests in peace studies were. This process seemed to aid students with "settling in" and deciding what they wanted to accomplish in the course; their learning thus became more self-directed.

A third reason for using service-learning in the course was to help students understand the stereotyping and depersonalization that often precede conflict (people become, for example, "the Bosnian Muslims" or "the Viet Cong," not individuals). Many students entered service-learning with stereotypes about the clients with whom they would be working. A young man doing service in a nursing home, for example, was surprised at the relationship he developed with an elderly man with whom he played checkers and at the man's depth of feeling for his wife, who was in another institution with a heart ailment. A young woman began to distinguish between the clients at a soup kitchen — the elderly couple who always waited politely and put trays away, the father with a rambunctious small daughter, the young man who was dressed the same way she was, in a T-shirt and jeans, who "looked as if he didn't need it." Similarly, just as students learned to differentiate among the clients of an agency, they also found that the staff and other workers at the agencies became individuals, and the complexities of social relationships, of meeting needs, and of making decisions became apparent to them.

Asking the students to see parallels of this complexity and of the differences between individuals, regardless of the group to which they nominally belonged (client, agency volunteer, staff), in larger organizations or nations was not difficult. The students' experience with service-learning (and the researchers' vicarious experience of it, through quarterly class reports by the service-learners) allowed them to see firsthand how stereotyping springs from ignorance but can be manipulated to accentuate differences and to exacerbate conflict. The issue of stereotyping was also addressed during the first night of class, when each student had to talk to someone in the class whom he or she did not know and then, both orally and in writing, had to introduce the person to me and to his or her classmates. Students discovered, for example, "He looks like a jock, but he's a religion major," and realized that their first impressions might not be adequate.

A fourth reason for having students engage in service-learning was to introduce them to some of the principles of intercultural communication. For an 18- or 19-year-old from a middle-class family, surrounded by 9,000 other young people, spending an afternoon at a nursing home or with a family in a homeless shelter can be, in some ways, like entering another culture. Misunderstandings can arise simply because people have different values and different ideas about how the world works. Early in the semester the class played an intercultural simulation game, "Barnga" (Thiagarajan and Steinwachs 1990), and discussed some of the emotions that typify an intercultural encounter: anxiety, disconfirmed expectancies (being upset not because something is intrinsically bad but because it's different from what one expected), lack of belonging (being an outsider), ambiguity (not knowing what is the right thing to say or do in the new culture), and confrontation with one's own prejudice (recognizing that one has treated those different from oneself by categorizing or stereotyping, and coming to terms with that when one has to interact with them as individuals) (Brislin 1986: 39-40). The service-learning students discussed and wrote about whether or not and how they experienced these emotions while in their service placements.

They also explored how such emotions could be manipulated to initiate or exacerbate conflict between cultures on a national scale.

Related both to stereotyping and to intercultural communication is the fifth reason for using service-learning in a peace studies course: examining the process of identity formation. As noted above, stereotyping and depersonalization often precede conflict. People do not go to war against John or Ivan or Ali or Jose; they go to war against a group that can be labeled "them" and not "us." But how do people come to identify with different groups? Consider, for example, a woman we can call Melody. She identifies herself as a secretary when she is at work; as a student when she goes to an evening class; as a mother when she tries to discipline her recalcitrant 12-year-old; as an African American when she offers advice and support to the African-American students in the department at the college in which she works; as a woman when, walking alone, she hears footsteps in the college parking lot late at night; and as a writer and a born-again Christian when she works on a book giving Christian advice to African-American women. She does not stop being a mother when she is sitting in her evening class, but it's not the identity she is aware of at that moment. At different times, different identities achieve prominence for her, and some of those identities can be politicized: turned into group action for the financial or political benefit of that group. For example, her identity as a secretary can become politicized if the college has a clerical workers' union that goes on strike, so the clerical workers see themselves as "us" and the administration becomes "them."

Students in the peace studies class were asked to explore how they become aware of different identities — from the ubiquitous government forms asking about their racial identities to cultural expectations of different roles (oldest son, little sister, student, athlete, and the like). Those in the service-learning cohort also were asked to reflect, in their journals, on how they became aware of new identities — agency volunteer, as opposed to staff or client; "young person" or "healthy person" or, to their surprise, "rich person," in the perception of clients at nursing homes, homeless shelters, or soup kitchens.

Identity almost always presupposes difference: difference between ages, between races, between genders, between socioeconomic classes, between whatever the constructed identity category and its opposite number or numbers are. Difference, in turn, can be manipulated to mean "wrong." In Japanese, for example, the same word has both of these meanings (Lustig and Koester 1993: 167, citing William Bohnaker). And the "wrong," different, "other" person then can be someone one is in conflict with — not individually, but as a representative of the group with which he or she is identified. Students saw slides of people in the (then) Soviet Union and examined how the same people could be made to seem as "us" or as "other," depending upon whether the people were identified (to put it simplistically) as "students" or "Communists." The "other" category is one with whom conflict is possible; the "us" category is someone in the "in-group," with whom we feel commonality, with whom we are at peace. A fifth reason to use service-learning in a peace studies class, then, is to help students understand how identity categories are created, to see how they come to identify with one group and not another, and to reflect upon the social construction and manipulation of identity: to reflect on what in society, what in history, what in literature, what in university life, for example, makes them think that race, on the one hand, is a valid identity and that being brown-eyed, on the other hand, is not.

Implications and Recommendations

Incorporating service-learning into a course adds a degree of complexity to teaching, but it also adds valuable learning to the course that would be difficult to replicate with other methods of teaching. In addition to helping me to meet the five course goals discussed above, service-learning, although messier and less conclusive when contrasted with more traditional approaches, seems to engender more thoughtful analysis, raising for students questions that do not end when the course ends. My evidence for this is anecdotal, but it suggests some avenues to pursue.

1. Students made four class presentations, each with an accompanying paper. Those in the research cohort gave more organized papers, with more traditional scholarship, but with less personal involvement, less self-examination, and, in general, less perception of shades of grey and fewer unanticipated questions than did those in the service-learning cohort. The discussion period following class presentations usually was longer following the service-learning presentations, as the presentations seemed to me to connect with personal issues that were meaningful to students. (My perceptions, of course, are colored by my own experience, which includes my socialization into my gender's roles and the value I therefore put on personalizing learning [Belenky et al. 1997]). This was despite the fact that the class presentations actually "counted" five percentage points more in grading for the research students than for the service-learning students, who had a greater variety of assignments to complete.

2. Unexpected learning for service-learning students — unexpected for them, and thus causing new thinking and reflection — included:

a. The young man who worked at the nursing home, and befriended an elderly man, began to think about his identity as a male and why that bonded him to an older person with whom he otherwise had little in common, while we discussed identity issues.

b. A young woman was startled to discover that her perceptions of the soup kitchen where she and another student worked were quite different from his, and this brought home to her the idea of cultural differences in perception in a way that reading and discussion had not.

c. A student who had served at a women's shelter for a number of months before the class began was surprised at how much more she understood about the agency, and thus how much more effective she could be, when she began to combine her action with structured reflection.

d. A journalism major, initially ecstatic at getting from the White House, where her mother worked, the donation of a used computer for the homeless shelter for which she was designing publicity materials, was surprised and irritated as the process, from initial decision to actual receipt, dragged on past the end of the semester. She and another journalism major also discovered that the director of the center was overburdened, that there were ethical choices about clients' privacy rights to be made, and that everything in a tiny shelter with a minimal budget takes a long time to achieve. They both decided to continue their involvement after the semester ended.

Although I believe that service-learning added to the students' learning in the course by raising questions and making connections between abstract ideas and the reality of people's lives in a way that traditional library research does not, I nevertheless would still change some parts of the class. (On a personal level, I should note that I accepted another position and had to begin traveling to New York before the semester ended, which obviously impinged on my effectiveness.) Here are some recommendations that might be appropriate for wider consideration.

1. To some extent, service placements were dictated by schedules and by access to transportation, a problem in a rural community. For future classes, I might explore car-pooling or find out more about bus routes, to give students more flexibility in choosing placements that really were what they wanted. Also, the students at the homeless shelter had very little client contact. The director needed publicity and fundraising materials, and producing those was intriguing initially to the two journalism students who chose to work there. After the day they spent at the shelter interviewing clients (and perhaps as well after listening to others in their cohort describe interactions with clients), they became dissatisfied with service that involved working alone at a computer (although both agreed to work on projects that continued past the end of the semester). While that dissatisfaction, too, provided learning, greater client contact might have permitted greater and different learning.

2. The reflection portion of the course, comprising the "Profile of an Agency" assignments along with the journal writing, worked well in general, but needed more time. Students found it difficult to do the service, read for

class, prepare for class presentations, and do the reflection as well. In addition, different sections of the Profile required different amounts of work from students: The women's shelter, for example, had a pamphlet with its mission statement clearly elucidated. Students working at the homeless shelter, on the other hand, had to interview the director and board members to gather the same information.

3. Relationships with supervisors at the service sites and their roles in evaluation should have been more clearly defined in my syllabus. Students interacted more with the director of service-learning, with whom they had an ongoing relationship, than with me. Again, the realities of agency people with busy schedules and professors with busy schedules intrude. Can you visit every agency where every student is placed? Ideally, yes. In reality, usually not.

Every peace studies educator has goals for student learning. If those goals include personalizing the learning and getting at questions that students will think about long after the semester is over, as well as unifying the content of the course, accommodating different learning styles, undercutting a tendency to stereotype, introducing concepts of intercultural communication, and exploring identity formation, then service-learning is an excellent way to help students reach those goals.

References

Belenky, Mary F., Blythe M. Clinchy, Nancy R. Goldberger, and Jill M. Tarule. (1997, reissue of the 1986 original). *Women's Ways of Knowing.* New York: Basic Books/Harper-Collins.

Brislin, Richard W. (1986). *Intercultural Interactions: A Practical Guide.* Newbury Park, CA: Sage Publications.

Lustig, Myron W., and Jolene Koester. (1993). *Intercultural Competence.* New York: Harper-Collins College Publishers.

Thiagarajan, Sivasasailam, and Barbara Steinwachs. (1990). *Barnga: A Simulation Game on Cultural Clashes.* Yarmouth, ME: Intercultural Press.

Walvoord, Barbara. Writing Across the Curriculum Workshop, Radford University, October 1994. (Dr. Walvoord, then a professor in the English department at the University of Cincinnati, now heads the Kaneb Center for Teaching and Learning at the University of Notre Dame.)

PEACE AND WORLD SECURITY STUDIES 200
Syllabus

TEXT

Barash, David P. Introduction to Peace Studies. Belmont, CA: Wadsworth Publishing Company, 1991

COURSE GOALS

(If you have different goals, or additional goals, see me about designing an individualized learning contract that will help you meet your goals.)

1. Students will be able to define war and peace, as the concepts make sense to them.
2. Students will be able to distinguish between "negative peace" and "positive peace."
3. Students will be able to list and discuss various ideas about what causes war.
4. Students will be able to list and discuss various ideas about what brings about peace.
5. Students will gain an understanding of how developments leading to war and those bringing about peace are played out in at least one nation other than the United States.
6. Students will examine their own ways of categorizing people as similar to or different from themselves, and will consider how such categorizing could contribute the causes of war.
7. Students will be able to discuss some concepts of intercultural communication, and will consider how intercultural misunderstandings could lead to or exacerbate conflict.
8. Students will make individual choices about ways of addressing issues of war and peace in their own lives.
9. Students will examine the links between interpersonal violence and group violence.
10. Students will develop skills in critical reading and listening: evaluating written materials and lectures, summarizing, linking course materials to their own concerns, etc.
11. Students will develop skills for working effectively in small groups.

TWO TRACKS: ACTIVIST AND RESEARCH

People in the Peace Studies field often are divided into two groups: activists and researchers. In this class, you will have an opportunity to choose one of the two roles.

Activist track:

Activist students will work at least an hour a week as a volunteer in a local social service agency. They will keep journals in which they reflect upon issues such as what makes them feel different from the clients of the agency and what connects them to those clients. These students also will write a series of papers titled, overall, "Profile of an Agency." In these papers, students will examine questions such as: Why does this agency exist? What is its mission? What are the demographics of the clients (age, gender, income, education, etc.)? Are there other agencies which serve this same population? Why does this population need this service? etc. Students will meet with others following the activist (service-learning) track and will make group presentations to the rest of the class.

Research track:

Research students will chose a country other than the United States and will examine how some of the issues we are considering -- for example, nuclear weapons, the existence of peace movements, human rights, etc. -- are manifested in that country. Alternatively, students may chose a particular conflict and examine how these issues apply to that conflict. These students will start by providing basic information on the country or the countries involved in the conflict (e.g. Where is it? What is its population? What is its per capita income? What are some key events in its history? What are some of the cultural attributes of its population?). They then will chose certain topics we are studying and investigate those topics as they relate to their chosen country or conflict. Students will meet with others in the research track and will make group presentations to the rest of the class.

COHORT GROUPS

Students will form two cohort groups: one for the students doing research and one for those doing service-learning. Four times during the semester, the groups will present what they have learned, so that the research people have the benefit of the activists' learning and vice versa. Students should function as a support group, an information resource, and a network for each other; you all should gain from each other's learning. An additional purpose of the group work is so that you can experience what it is like to negotiate over something which is important to you --your academic work -- with other people who have some common interests but also perhaps some different agendas. This will give you an idea of what diplomats and other negotiators go through in trying to reach solutions to problems of conflict. I will schedule meeting times in class for the cohort groups, but plan to be in touch by e-mail or phone also. You may need more than the scheduled time.

READING SUMMARIES AND COMMENTARIES

This class will NOT be a lecture class, except possibly when we have guest lecturers. (The instructions which follow apply even when we have guest lecturers!) You will be expected to do the reading IN ADVANCE of class and come ready to discuss the material. Note that you don't need to read all assignments in the same way; you read different materials for different purposes. I will try to let you know what I would like you to get out of a particular reading, but you should think through your own purposes as well. To facilitate class discussion, by Tuesday evening you should:

1. e-mail or fax or deliver or mail to me (so that I have it by Tuesday evening) your summary of the readings for this week (one paragraph for each reading)

2. e-mail to the rest of the class (we will get a class alias) a comment on the reading, a paragraph or so long, such as:

   - What I didn't understand about this reading was....
   - I thought that the author's reasoning was weak when he/she said....
   - When the author wrote about ___ I was reminded of ___ (something else you have read or experienced)...
   - It seems to me that another interpretation of this would be....
   - This author seems to disagree with what our guest lecturer said last week on these points...
   - What this author says really only applies to the U.S. and Western Europe. In the country I'm studying, people might react this way
   - What the author describes is different from what I'm experiencing in my service placement....
   - I tried to apply this to what I read in the news yesterday. This is what I figured out...
   - I agree/disagree with [another student's] comment on the reading, because....

STUDENT EVALUATION

In freshman and sophomore-level courses, you should expect to do two hours of work outside of class for every hour you spend in class. (For junior and senior level classes, expect three to four hours of work outside of class for each hour in class.) I am anticipating that you will spend approximately six hours per week outside of class on this course, divided as follows:

2 hours	reading (approximately 50 pages per week)
1 hour	summary writing and posting reading commentary
3 hours	activist (service-learning) or research work

If you find that course work is taking you longer than this, bring that up in class. The important thing is to meet the course goals and your goals, and we can negotiate how to do that.

Your grade in the course will be based on the following (unless you and I design an individualized learning contract which specifies another method of evaluation):

1.	Summaries of your reading each week.	10%
2.	Commentary on the readings posted to the class by e-mail.	10%
3.	Class participation.	10%
4.	Participation in your cohort group.	10%
5.	Final essay.	10%

Activist (service-learning) students:

1.	The quality of your reflective journal (graded on a +, check, - basis).	10%
2.	Your "Profile of an Agency" papers.	10%
3.	Your work at your service site.	10%
4.	The quality of your class presentations.	20%

Research students:

1.	The quality of your research papers.	25%
2.	The quality of your class presentations.	25%

Hunger for Justice:
Service-Learning in Feminist/Liberation Theology

by Michele James-Deramo

How do we engage students in an analysis of the injustices of poverty, racism, and political oppression that includes a careful examination of their own life-styles and attitudes? In particular, how do we invite white, middle-class students to consider how their life-styles might contribute to the persistence of these problems and how they, as inheritors of the dominant culture, need to both effect change *and* change themselves?

The Primary Objective: Critical Self-Examination

It was this habit of critical self-examination that I wanted to foster in my students when I was working as the director of service-learning in the Faith-Justice Institute at Saint Joseph's University (SJU), Philadelphia. The institute was founded in 1977 in response to the universal charge of the 32nd General Congregation of the Society of Jesus that the service of faith and the promotion of justice should be the integrating factor of all Jesuit ministries (Padberg 1977: 9). The mission of the institute was to advance this call of faith through justice by providing the university with an academic forum that probed questions of peace and justice through coursework, lectures, field placements, and a certificate program that enabled students to add a peace-justice concentration to their major coursework. Although not formally a peace studies program, the Faith-Justice Certificate addressed the interplay of economic, sociocultural, and political issues; explored our moral response to these issues; and provided a theological context from which to reflect critically and act.

I was planning to teach the interdisciplinary faith-justice course, Hunger for Justice (INT 3001), and was searching for the right content to shape this rather open-ended course on doing justice from a faith perspective. I had recently discovered Sharon Welch's text, *A Feminist Ethic of Risk,* which spoke directly to the questions of how oppressed communities sustained energy, hope, and commitment in the face of an unrelenting succession of social and political crises and, conversely, how good people from more affluent communities were prevented from effectively responding to serious social and political crises (1990: 1-2). Welch's text provided a systematic plan for working through these and other related questions, eventually leading to the formation of an ethic that supported risk taking from within a heritage of hope and commitment. Further, Welch's perspective reflected that of most of the students at SJU: She spoke honestly from the point of view of a white, middle-class woman accustomed to material comforts and personal achievement. From within her perspective she challenged the "cultured despair" of the middle class, a despair "cushioned by privilege and grounded in privilege" that prevents long-term social change, since the good life is already accessible or within reach for one's self and family (1990: 15). Welch's text provided the academic resource needed to guide students through a process of critical self-examination and reflection on action, so I adopted the text as the centerpiece of the course.

I envisioned this interdisciplinary service-learning course as a capstone for third-level students completing the Faith-Justice Certificate program. The service-learning initiative, an option for fulfilling the certificate program, was a three-tiered sequence of courses that loosely reflected the developmental schema proposed by William Perry (1970). Each level of coursework was rooted in the university's core curriculum and informed by the school's Jesuit tradition. The goal of the service was not only to meet community needs but also to draw students into a "preferential option for the poor," an approach that entails a decision to act on behalf of and make as a priority the liberation of the poor from the conditions of their poverty (Segundo 1976). Third-level students, generally juniors and seniors, developed a theological framework for action that reflected and supported their personal commitment to social justice. The service work at this level engaged the students as participants in a community that shared a common goal, vision, and purpose. In other words, students would no longer act *on behalf of,* but would act *with* others. (See the syllabus at the end of this essay.) Unfortunately, my plans for the course did not unfold as anticipated. Due to curriculum constraints, I taught INT 3001 as a Directed Readings course for two students. Nevertheless, I learned a great deal from the experience that I hope will be fruitful for others, as well.

The Course Design: Essential Questions and Necessary Actions

As the primary text for the course, Welch's *A Feminist Ethic of Risk* provided the outline for our work in the class. Each week we explored a single chapter from the book. I prepared weekly discussion guides that identified two or three objectives for the week, followed by essential questions drawn from the text. (See samples at the end of this essay.) I bulleted key ideas I wanted to explore and followed these bulleted points with italicized questions that aimed to link the concept with the student's own experience. For example, in the initial class lesson, Good and Evil in the Nuclear World: When Good Intentions Bear Evil Consequences, the class objectives were:

- to determine the lens through which we examine the course material,
- to name the assumptions and perspectives that guide our action, and
- to begin the process of critically examining our own good intentions.

The essential questions were:

- What causes good people to participate in, for example, the nuclear arms race?
- What blocks effective resistance to social evils?

The subsequent reflection question was:

Choose a crisis that you address through your social action, for example, violence against women. Use this as a lens through which you study the patterns of morality and rationality that underlie this crisis and allow it to continue.

This kind of question was generally followed by invitations for students to consider attitudes and beliefs learned from their *own* communities of origin that reinforced or challenged the underlying assumptions of their particular social crises. Obviously, students confronting these questions for the first time would not be able to identify readily the patterns of thought or underlying beliefs that shaped their course of action. Therefore, I built in opportunities for students to revisit their earlier reflections and revise or develop what they had written.

Throughout her text, Welch draws upon the literary tradition of contemporary African-American women writers such as Paule Marshall (1984), Toni Morrison (1970), Toni Cade Bambara (1981), and Mildred Taylor (1983, 1984). Welch uses selected works by these authors to illustrate the moral wisdom underlying an ethic of risk, and applies the interpretive method of ethicist Katie Cannon (1988) for understanding the literature. Reading literature by contemporary African-American authors proved to be an important element of the course. Not only did these texts enlarge students' context beyond their own experience but they also helped make Welch's ideas accessible. Characters such as Merle Kimbona (Marshall 1984), Pecola Breedlove (Morrison 1970), Cassie Logan (Taylor 1983), and Velma Henry (Bambara 1981) were real. They embodied lifetimes of experience that mirrored the lives of the communities with which the students worked — though their presence was not always apparent owing to the limited and sometimes artificial nature of the service-learning encounter. The artificial nature of certain service-learning encounters results, I believe, from the fact that students are not fully engaged in the communities in which they work. Not only have these students grown up in neighborhoods and schools that are vastly different from their placement sites but they also frequently live in the insular community of the college campus. Consequently, service-learners move in and out of people's lives, imagining that they know the people with whom they are working, when in fact this knowledge is largely superficial and narrowly focused on a particular issue or problem.

In addition to enlarging the community context through literature, I wanted to broaden students' exposure to men and women who are examples of moral courage. I wanted students to see that social change was possible and to discover through the narratives of these moral heroes the motivations for continuing on their path despite seemingly insurmountable obstacles and, quite frequently, the threat of bodily harm. I assigned the book *Cloud of Witnesses* (Hollyday and Wallis 1991) as a secondary text. This text compiled interviews with peace and justice activists, such as Dom Helder Camara, Albertina Sisulu, and Myles Horton, that originally appeared in *Sojourners* magazine. Although this was not an academic text per se, it did provide a broad introduction to various historical movements and some of the key players in those movements. Furthermore, the common language of these articles offered a refreshing balance to the rich, metaphorical language of the novels and the Welch text. Students could find their own voice for reflection modeled in these narratives.

Service-learning was a natural component of the course. However, coordination of an appropriate service experience was difficult to achieve. I wanted students to be a part of a community that was seriously and intensively involved in some kind of social change activity. I imagined that students might spend time at a Catholic Worker house in north Philadelphia and participate in the outreach activities of that particular house of hospitality, or join forces with an urban neighborhood organization engaged in community revitalization efforts. The students needed to be in regular contact with grass-roots leadership. Further, they needed to relinquish the typical community service role of "helper" and assume an authentic partner relationship with the group or organization with which they were involved. Ideally, the service would be a natural extension of work the students had been doing for a year or more prior to the course, in which case they would already be acclimated to the goals of the community and know the key players.

To achieve this kind of interaction, it was necessary for me to be flexible. For example, I did not require students to be at their site weekly at a designated hour; nor did I require that a site supervisor be identified who could evaluate the students' performance at the end of the semester. These sorts of requirements, while important in other kinds of courses, would have constrained natural affiliations with the community and kept the students as outsiders. Instead, I chose to rely upon the quality and depth of the students' weekly reflections as evidence that they were meeting their 40-hour minimum service requirement and were sufficiently engaged in substantive work with the community.

What Really Happened

As noted above, the course became a Directed Readings for two students. If the actual classroom experience was not what I had expected, then neither were the two students who enrolled. (Names and identifying characteristics have been eliminated in the discussion that follows.)

"T" was a traditional-age student, raised in a white, middle-class Catholic home. Although she seemed to fit the profile of the typical SJU student, she was actually quite removed from the affluence of many of her peers. She was a commuter to campus, traveling approximately 30 to 40 minutes in Philadelphia traffic to get to school each day. In addition to being a full-time student, T was waitressing close to 40 hours a week in order to pay her college tuition. Given this combination of commuting from a distant suburb and working almost full-time in the evenings, T was unable to participate fully in the social side of campus life. Consequently, she had little contact with the school's Homeless Coalition, which included some of the school's most active and articulate student leaders, even though she was committed to working with women living in shelters and managed to complete an in-depth psychology internship with one of the shelter networks in the city.

The other student, "B," an African-American man in his 40s, was a pastor of a nondenominational Christian church and resident of a local North Philadelphia community. While B's academic plan was to complete his degree in marketing, he was committed to the work of the Faith-Justice Institute. A friendly and somewhat ingenuous man, B liked to visit my office for long conversations. He often praised my efforts to get students to think about social justice. B's role as a community leader with the O. Neighbors Against Drugs (ONAD) neighborhood organization best exemplified the model of service that I had hoped to inculcate in the Hunger for Justice students.

I mention these details because the personal circumstances of my two students contributed enormously to the dynamics of the "class" and how it unfolded. In addition to their academic work, both students had many responsibilities that competed for their time and attention. Yet, both clearly possessed a desire to be engaged in the hard work of social change.

T wrote about the grim face of a shelter manager who had seen hundreds of abused and neglected women and children pass through the door. When recounting a conversation with this woman, T struggled with the woman's resigned cynicism. At the same time, T recognized that a daily confrontation with human suffering is disempowering to even the most committed activists; therefore, the presence of a supportive community with whom one can mourn the losses and celebrate the small victories was essential. The importance of community was felt by T on a personal level, as well. Her own initiatives with the shelter network had been done independently, without the support of a class or an organization of like-minded peers. Even her family and boyfriend questioned her continued involvement in such "depressing" work.

B wrote about his organization's efforts to eliminate drug trafficking in their neighborhood and the challenge of balancing effective and organized resistance with the personal safety of the group. Discussion on the meaning of responsible action and how this is defined by one's community was particularly relevant in his situation. ONAD focused primarily on activism, sponsoring a Neighborhood Watch and organizing marches and rallies. However, the group also wanted to raise funds to renovate a donated warehouse as a community center that would offer recreational and educational activities to local children and youth.

B tended to demonize drug dealers and regarded drug addiction as a moral flaw, even though he was aware of the economic and social realities that were at the root of such problems. Interestingly, one of the most enlightening discussions for B was when we discussed structural sin and its subsequent effect of internalized self-hatred. We were reading Morrison's novel, The Bluest Eye, and contemplating the rape of Pecola Breedlove by her father. Pecola's father was a man who had grown up as an orphan, knowing only grinding poverty and racial humiliation. Because Breedlove was raised in an environment deficient in love on so many levels, he was morally limited as an actor in the world. Consequently, he could only hand on to his daughter the legacy of the great wrong that had been done to him. This piece enabled B to see that the far-reaching, destructive effects of structural sin included an impediment to love that can contribute to victims preying on other victims. Conversely, poor and oppressed people whose lives are rich in love — such as the Logan family depicted in Mildred Taylor's novels — are better equipped to confront their oppression and resist it creatively.

T's participation in the faith-justice course brought her outside of her familiar realm of the comfortable, working middle class. When she went to the shelter, despite her years of prior involvement, she remained a person with a car, a credit card, and a college degree, who could leave at any time. Even though her acquisition of the degree was not an easy one, T nonetheless benefited from her middle-class status and the opportunities it afforded her. For T, the struggle was overcoming the loneliness of working for justice outside of her community of origin and discovering solidarity with people who shared her values and history.

On the other hand, B's work was done from within his community. When B went to an ONAD meeting, he stayed in his own neighborhood. B's teenage daughter and other youths living in his neighborhood were vulnerable to the immanent violence and temptations of the drug trade that threatened their neighborhood with deterioration. Even though many of the youths in B's neighborhood were among the working class, they did not enjoy the security of their suburban peers. At any unpredictable moment, a stray bullet or wrong-headed association could steal away their opportunity forever. Thus, B's participation in the course brought an element of reality and a degree of urgency to the protected environment of the college classroom. I remember how B's eyes would dance because *people in the university were finally discussing the issues that surrounded him every day* in North Philadelphia.

Evaluation

T and B came to the class from distinct historical locations, yet both were significantly engaged in social change. For these students, the course was an opportunity to take their voluntarism a step further into the realm of service-learning. Both students recognized the role of faith-based communities in motivating them to service; however, neither had reflected upon how these communities shaped their current attitudes or defined their strategies for responding to social crises. Through literature, service, and personal narrative, integrated as service-learning, they better realized their own heritages of belief as well as their mutual interplay. The Welch text set forth a series of provocative questions that challenged all of us in this process. Both students indicated that the intimate class setting allowed them to grapple openly with complex ideas and that this was helpful in their own integration of the material.

The Welch text may have been too advanced for undergraduates with minimal theological training. Although it was a valuable resource, I probably would not assign it again as students' primary reading. Instead, I would present Welch's key ideas predominantly through literature and give greater attention to narratives such as those in the Wallis-Hollyday text. The students learned concepts from Welch that provoked them to think more deeply. However, I am not certain that their understanding of these concepts was integrated with their self-reflection or their existing decisions for how and why to act.

But then, this sort of integration is a life's work.

References

Bambara, Toni Cade. (1981). *The Salt Eaters*. New York, NY: Vintage Books.

Cannon, Katie. (1988). *Black Womanist Ethics*. Atlanta, GA: Scholars Press.

Hollyday, Joyce, and Jim Wallis, eds. (1991). *Cloud of Witnesses*. Maryknoll, NY: Orbis Books.

Marshall, Paule. (1984). *The Chosen Place, The Timeless People*. New York, NY: Random House.

Morrison, Toni. (1970). *The Bluest Eye*. New York, NY: Holt, Rinehart and Winston.

Padberg, John W., S.J, ed. (1977). "Jesuits Today." In *Documents of the 31st and 32nd General Congregations of the Society of Jesus*, 9. St. Louis, MO: Institute of Jesuit Sources.

Perry, William G., Jr. (1970). *Forms of Intellectual and Ethical Development in the College Years: A Scheme*. New York, NY: Holt, Rinehart and Winston.

Segundo, Juan Luis. (1976). *Liberation of Theology*. Translated by John Drury. Maryknoll, NY: Orbis Books.

Taylor, Mildred. (1983). *Let the Circle Be Unbroken*. New York, NY: Bantam Books.

——— . (1984). *Roll of Thunder, Hear My Cry*. New York, NY: Bantam Books.

Welch, Sharon. (1990). *A Feminist Ethic of Risk*. Minneapolis, MN: Fortress Press.

INT 3001: HUNGER FOR JUSTICE

Description:

How can we maintain our commitment to justice in the face of unrelenting social and political crises?

This course draws upon the rich resources of social history, resistance literature and liberation thought in order to create an ethic of sustained action that is essential to the work of justice. Adopting a seminar format, this course will engage you in cross-cultural dialogue, reflection on your own form of social outreach, and creative response to the problems of injustice.

The first section of the course will draw upon the literary tradition of contemporary African-American women writers. Our interpretation of these texts will follow the method of ethicist Katie G. Cannon, whose book, Black Womanist Ethics, describes "the moral wisdom found in black women's literary tradition."

The second section of the course will construct a theology of resistance and hope, from which an ethic of risk may flow. The primary text for the course, A Feminist Ethic of Risk, by Sharon Welch, will provide the outline for our work. Welch's work will be supplemented by excerpts from other feminist, liberation and political theologians.

Throughout the course, you will be called upon to address personally the questions at hand. What does this mean for your life? To whom do you look for examples of strength, courage and sustained action? The text, Cloud of Witnesses, edited by activists Jim Wallis and Joyce Hollyday, will assist you in seeking mentors for sustained social action.

Finally, you will be asked to look within and broaden your own base of experience through a 40 hour community service project. Perhaps the best way to wrestle with the difficult questions presented in the course is through compelling encounters with people who are coping with social and political crises in their daily lives.

Requirements:

Attendance
Although this is a directed readings course, we will meet ten times during the semester. During that time we will grapple with significant questions arising from the readings. Your attendance at these meetings is required. If illness of personal circumstances prevent you from attending a session, please inform me as soon as possible so that we may reschedule the meeting. Class attendance accounts for 10% of your final grade.

INT 3001: HUNGER FOR JUSTICE

Service Project

As a part of your service project, you will complete a service-learning agreement using a standard form provided for you. The service-learning agreement must be completed prior to your service placement and should be approved by a representative from the site. The service-learning agreement clarifies and focuses your responsibilities at the site.

You are expected to complete at least 40 hours of service work at your site. The work should be completed incrementally over a twelve week period.

At the conclusion of your service term, your site supervisor will complete an evaluation of your work using the service-learning agreement as a gauge for assessing your performance. The overall service project, including timely completion of the service-learning agreement and fulfillment of the service hours, accounts for 30% of your final grade.

Reflection Papers

The course content aims to engage you both intellectually and personally. Reflection and reanalysis papers of 3 - 4 pages in length are required at various points throughout the course. These papers are designed to stimulate a critical examination of your assumptions and facilitate a deeper analysis and conscious construction of your chosen system of belief. Reflection and reanalysis papers account for 30% of your grade.

Integrative Project

A central theme of the course is that we cannot be moral alone. Your integrative project invites you to explore this idea more fully in the following way:

Define the nature of the community from which you derive hope, sustenance and a sense of heritage.

- How does this community define responsible action?
- How does it perceive its work in the world in relation to the work of God?
- How does this community provide you with a sense of solidarity and common purpose? With a sense of belonging to a heritage of resistance?
- How has your involvement with the community at your site influenced your perception of your own community?

Use the ideas presented in Welch as a framework for making your claims. The integrative project accounts for 30% of your final grade.

James-Deramo: 2

**PERSISTENCE IN THE FACE OF PARTIAL VICTORIES
AND CONTINUED DEFEATS**

Objectives:
- To understand the power dynamics that underlie "a failure of nerve";
- To grasp the essence of "risk" as it pertains to responsible action;
- To begin to locate new sources of wisdom to empower our responsible action.

Essential Questions:

Cultured Despair of the Middle Class
- Cultured despair is predicated on material comfort and security, as well as an ethos of individualism.

    How is this attitude of cultured despair evident among your peers who also confront the social crises that you address in your service project?

Testimonies of Wisdom
- Conversely, "sheer holy boldness" (Cannon) is predicated on fierce whimsy (acting without guarantee of success) and a grounding in community.

    Who among your peers represents this "sheer holy boldness"? What is the source of this boldness?

- Welch and Cannon both emphasize that we cannot romanticize testimonies of resistance without also knowing the costs of such resistance.

    How does this reality of the costs suffered fit into our understanding of an ethic of risk?
    Is it possible to cultivate an ethic of risk without an acceptance of suffering?

For Our Next Class:

Write a 2 - 3 page essay describing your social action, how you were drawn to this action, what you hope to accomplish through your service project and how you see yourself as an actor in the larger struggle.

We will discuss these essays in light of our next set of readings on the ethic of control and persuasiveness of the control ethic -- even among peace activists.

A HERITAGE OF PERSISTENCE, IMAGINATION AND SOLIDARITY: HOW MUCH HAS BEEN LOST?

Objectives:
- To discuss the concept of the "great wrong" as a theological concept depicting deep spiritual crisis;
- To grasp the depth of loss occurring as a result of structural sin.

Essential Questions:

- Welch states that with an ethic of risk, "action begins in the face of overwhelming loss and the recognition of the irreparable damage of structural evil."

  What is the appropriate response to overwhelming loss? Why is such a response "risky"?

- In Morrison's novel, <u>The Bluest Eye</u>, the "great wrong" is characterized as internalized self hatred that causes victims to hurt other victims.

  In this story, how could a person undo the great wrong that destroys Pecola Breedlove? What would you do?

- Welch claims that the work required to redress the great wrong is the work of generations; that "goodwill, money, and new ideas" will not alter the structural evil.

  What does this say about the role of justice in the lives of morally mature individuals? In this context, why wouldn't "goodwill, money and new ideas" be regarded as just methods?

For Our Next Class:

Write a short essay describing the conflict faced by your community and how your community creatively resisted the evil inherent in that conflict.

HOW MUCH HAS SURVIVED?
A DISCUSSION OF CREATIVE RESISTANCE

Objectives:
- To define "responsible action" through a delineation of limits;
- To understand the breadth of "creative resistance" -- as a way to maintain self-respect, as well as a means of confronting / resisting evil nonviolently.

Essential Questions:

- Welch writes that responsible action does not entail one individual resolving the problems of others. Rather, it entails changing what can be altered in the present, and establishing the conditions for further (partial) change by others.

  Given these parameters, what is the challenge of responsible action? What particular challenges to responsible action do you face in your work for social change?

- The Logans are a family that models responsible action within a very restrained context. What are some of the lessons learned through their various forms of resistance?

  1. Mama's work as a teacher *(An "insurrection of subjugated knowledge")*
  2. The pasted-over book covers *(Resisting the notion that we need to accept things the way they are)*
  3. Calling friends "Miss" after being forced to call a white girl "Miss" *(Knowing when to resist; undoing the indignity)*

  Describe your community's creative resistance.

For Our Next Class:

Our final classes will be reading intensive. Therefore, I ask that you prepare questions about what you read. We will work through these during our final sessions.

Begin outlining your final paper in light of the issues raised in class. The final chapters will help you to formulate a theological framework within which to address the question.

SERVICE-LEARNING CONTRACT

Name of Student_____

Address and Telephone Number During School Semester

_____

_____

Service-Learning Course_____

Community Service Site_____

Schedule of Service Hours: I agree to provide _____ hours of service a week for the entire semester/academic year beginning _____. My scheduled hours of service are: _____

Community Service Goals: My volunteer work at the above named organization includes:

While serving at this organization, my goal is:

Learning Goals: Through this experience I hope to learn:

Statements of Commitment

Student: I agree to fulfill to the best of my abilities the Service-Learning arrangements described above.

_____
Signature   Date

Site Supervisor: I agree to guide this student's work done under my direction and to complete a final evaluation of his/her efforts.

_____
Signature   Date

Faculty: I agree to award a grade to this student upon his/her satisfactory completion of the Service-Learning course.

_____
Signature   Date

Service-Learning in Methods of Peacemaking at Earlham College

by Howard Richards and Mary Schwendener-Holt

This essay examines service-learning within the context of a Peace and Global Studies course at Earlham College, a Quaker liberal arts college. Service-learning fits directly with the mission of the college, which emphasizes "pursuit of truth where ever that pursuit leads . . . respect for the consciences of others; openness to new truth . . . [and] application of what is known to improving our world," and also encourages students to be active learners and to develop "concern for the world in which we live" (Earlham College Mission Statement).

The Peace and Global Studies curriculum (PAGS) consists of four sets of interconnected courses. The first of the four sets is called "issues to structures." Its general aim is to move students from understanding social issues to understanding social structures. The second set is called "methods," which imparts practical peacemaking and justice-making skills. The third set of courses is off-campus experience, often in one of the programs specifically designated for PAGS off-campus study (Jerusalem, Belfast) or another suitable program. The fourth and final set of courses is called "methodology," which engages students in contemporary social theory and preparation for a senior thesis.

Methods of Peacemaking falls into the second set of courses. In addition to other PAGS courses (Conflict Resolution, Theory and Practice of Nonviolence), it is designed to provide students with practical tools for facilitating social change. It is generally taken in the second year, as a way of helping students find concrete ways to solve the problems studied in the first set of courses. It also functions as preparation for the off-campus experience. This course functions much as a laboratory course, with the agencies serving as social change laboratories.

Methods of Peacemaking

Methods of Peacemaking is a service-learning course on community development, the theory and practice of what Paulo Freire calls "cultural action," peace education, social science methodology, and *educacion popular*. Service-learning assignments occur over the entire semester. Placements occur in social settings in Richmond, Indiana, the town in which Earlham College is located. The service-learning component of the course provides a considerable degree of immersion in a particular Richmond scene and a relatively prolonged acquaintance with several local people. Placements have included the Boy's Club; Girls, Inc.; a senior day-care center; a neighborhood association; a food and clothing pantry; and a battered women's shelter.

Earlham College has a community service office, which consists of a service-learning coordinator and a student-run volunteer program called the Earlham Volunteer Exchange. In general, the office provides logistical support for students as they enter and work in the agencies. Some students have an ongoing service commitment before they take the Methods class, and they use the service they are already performing to meet the objectives of the class.

Students are expected to spend at least one hour per week during the 15-week semester at their service-learning site and to cross-check what they are learning about the local culture from other sources (including two other experiential course components that will be discussed below). They write a paper reporting on their service-learning experience, and they make an oral report to the class. The sharing of oral reports provides an opportunity for comparing findings. Discussions help students to reflect on their experiences in their service-learning placements. Additionally, students write a brief account of their service experience, and a longer autobiographical account of the experiences that have shaped who they are — an account in which service-learning is often an important component.

In addition to the service-learning experience, there are two other experiential components in Methods. One of these is a series of brief site visits that introduce students to various parts of the community, including labor unions, factories, veterans' organizations, farm co-ops, basketball games, hospitals, schools, bars, social clubs (like the Moose Lodge), and, most often, experiences related to religion, including black churches, Pentecostal revivals, mainline Protestant services, Catholic parishes, and the Knights of Columbus. The third experiential component of Methods is viewing elements of popular culture, most notably national television programs, which are beamed into the consciousness of Richmond from outside, and which — statistics tell us — occupy a major portion of its people's waking hours.

The students who take Methods are already committed to making a positive change in the world, thus the service-learning dovetails with their larger learning goals. The service opportunity, combined with the opportunity to reflect on their service with peers and the teacher, helps students to place the commitment they already have in a concrete context. Additionally, the course is designed to help students articulate the reasons for their commitment, and the influences in their lives that have led to it. Their ongoing experience at their service site provides a weekly dose of practice that provides a small but significant reality check for their ongoing effort to articulate their goals.

Students are prepared for combining service with learning in several ways. One is through completing a series of listening exercises, along the lines of "native language ethnographic interviews" (Spradley 1979). These exercises impart skills that students will practice both at their service-learning sites and in the many short site visits made by the class. Students divide into pairs and take turns listening to each other. The aim is to understand the other person's meaning, and to discern his or her emotions, with the least possible interference caused by interjecting one's own ideas and feelings. These exercises serve to introduce discussions of different approaches to interviewing and participant observation. They also start the students discussing their own present and future roles as "organic intellectuals," "learner teachers," "wounded healers," or "servant leaders" who might, at some point, run the risk of being designated by some less flattering title, such as "outside agitators." The question of one's role raises the question of the relationship between broad goals chosen in the light of a structural understanding of social problems informed by the findings of ecological and social science and the perceived immediate needs and concerns of people in the community.

The teacher participates more or less as an equal with the students in working to understand the local culture and in trying to relate to it in positive and constructive ways. The experiences are never the same from one year to the next, and the teacher, for the most part, assumes in discussion only what a particular class has discovered that year. The aim is not to seek a stable and verified body of knowledge that the teacher knows and the students learn. What the teacher brings to the investigative team is theoretical background and experience in doing social research both in Richmond and at other times and in other places. What the students learn are skills that will help them to be effective peacemakers wherever they may find themselves.

Theoretical Perspectives

From a theoretical point of view, the service-learning experience fits into the course in several ways. In order to introduce some of the theory informing the course, a succinct description of the philosophies of Antonio Gramsci and Paulo Freire, as they apply to this course, follows. It should be noted, however, that the ideas of these well-known philosophers of social change influenced the design of the course only indirectly. It was not their theories, but the senior author's experience in *educacion popular* programs at the Center for Research and Development in Education (CIDE) in Santiago, Chile, that led to the existence of the Methods course at Earlham. Freire and Gramsci were part of the theoretical background of the work done at CIDE, and the following account does not reflect so much the original texts of Gramsci and Freire as it does the ways in which their ideas have been interpreted and applied at CIDE.

The general aim of the service-learning project is "moral and intellectual reform" (a Gramscian concept). To accomplish the reform, it is necessary to move "from common sense to good sense" (Garcia-Huidobro 1979; Gramsci 1957). To establish the common sense of a given group, it is necessary to do a "codification of the thematic universe" (Freire 1997). To move from common sense toward good sense, it is necessary to seek and find "untested feasibilities" and "generative themes" (Freire 1997). For Freire, a "generative theme" is a unit of meaning usable in a consciousness-raising approach to literacy. In Chile, a "generative theme" could also be a *pauta social* [social norm] capable of generating social change.

The service-learning project helps students develop an understanding of the common sense of the people with whom they work at their service site. It also helps them to cross-check (triangulate) what they are learning about the common sense of Richmond through site visits and through thematic analysis of the media.

The Debriefings

One of the most distinctive features of Methods is a process called "debriefing." The debriefing format serves as an important opportunity to record and process the students' experiences in the site visits, with the media, and in their service-learning assignments. The debriefing process functions, in part, as a way of having students reflect on their service as it applies to creating what Freire would call a "codification of the thematic universe."

Debriefing should be done immediately after the experience to be debriefed. Good debriefing requires insightful interpretations and exploring feelings regarding interpersonal interactions. These are most effective when students' memories are fresh. Because we discourage note taking or recording during the experience, it is desirable to make notes immediately afterward before details are forgotten. This is especially important because we believe it is critical to write down what people say, instead of paraphrasing what we imagine to be their thoughts.

The first step in debriefing is called "insertion" *(insercion en la comunidad)*. The members of the team reflect on how well they were able to integrate themselves into the ongoing social reality defined by the time, place, setting, and cast of characters of the service-learning assignment (or site visit). This is a natural way to begin the debriefing because the students are usually somewhat self-conscious, and worry about whether they are making a good impression, whether people are disturbed by their presence, and whether people have changed their normal activities because of the presence of an outsider. This step provides occasions for discussing a number of theoretical and ethical issues. For example, students struggle with whether they should accept sexist, racist, homophobic, or other antidemocratic attitudes at their service-learning site, in order to do their social research more scientifically; or whether they should take a stand for ethical principles they believe in. The discussion of "insertion" allows students to compare and explore the experiences of others. Students work with the class to define their roles at their sites and to relate them to the objectives of the course.

The second step in debriefing is called "story." Students share the explanation they gave of their presence at the site. A person's story might have been that she was an Earlham College student who was offering to work at Girls, Inc. because she liked kids. Sometimes the story is implicit: The people around you assume you are an Earlham College student without having to be told; they assume that you are intelligent, that you are an idealist who is motivated to serve because of your religious background, and that you are at least prosperous, if not rich. This is a story that could be assigned to students without their saying a word, although they could revise it by talking about themselves. In the writing of the autobiographies, the idea of "story" broadens into exercises in which the students reflect on and develop the stories of their lives. The longer, autobiographical "story" helps students focus on understanding and articulating why peacemaking is a part of their life goals and why particular aspects of peace and justice (such as ecology issues or women's issues) motivate them. Discussions of "stories" often can lead to broader discussions about humans as creatures who live by myths; myth as a basis of language and culture; story sharing as a way of bonding; multiculturalism as telling the stories of those who have been forgotten by dominant mainstream stories; Thomas Berry's (1991) claim that "there is no community without a community story"; Thomas Groome's (1987) idea of religious education as "sharing our story and vision"; and social change as a process of story repair.

The next step in the debriefing process is called "names." Students examine whether they have learned the names of the people encountered during the service-learning or site visit. This is a step toward looking for ways to open up channels of communication, establishing a network of contacts, developing relationships, and finding what the Chilean activist Jorge Zuleta (Richards 1985) calls "generative persons" (personas generadoras). The generative person is someone in whom and through whom constructive social change is already taking place. These individuals may be helpful in getting any new "untested feasibility" under way, but may need some encouragement or help to persevere in what they are already doing. In the "names" part of debriefing, students relate the broad goal of peacemaking to building relationships with particular persons.

The fourth focus in debriefing involves "themes." A good way to introduce this topic is to give as an example a theme that Paulo Freire's team discovered when doing a codification of the thematic universe among peasants on a large Chilean farm called El Recurso. A theme in the life of the peasants of El Recurso was theft. Everyone there talked about thieves, suspected thieves, false accusations of theft, possible thefts, legendary thefts of the past, and actual thefts. Thus, theft was a theme in the life-world (the thematic universe) of that group of people in that place (Freire 1997). Among the themes that students have found in the life-worlds of one or another group in Richmond, Indiana, are racial violence and salvation.

The term "theme" can be traced back to the project for grounding all science in phenomenology undertaken at the turn of the century by Edmund Husserl (1931). Freire's "thematic universe" is similar to what Husserl (1970) called a "life-world" (Lebenswelt). When we study themes, we study Wilden's (1972) "meaning explanations." Meaning explanations apply to socially constructed realities. As a practical matter, we say that we have learned a theme when we can participate in its use. For example, if we could strike up a conversation about theft with Chilean peasants, or about salvation with Indiana Pentecostal church members, then we would know that we had "learned" these themes. Working with the themes that appear in their agencies helps students examine their service more closely. Additionally, it helps students connect the methodological issues in understanding groups with their agency placements.

The last step in debriefing is called "energy" or "energy insight." The choice of the word *energy* reflects a rapprochement of common sense and theory. At the level of common sense, students come to the class already familiar with ways the word *energy* is used. People derive "energy" from what motivates them. At the level of theory, Anthony Wilden (translator and expositor for Jacques Lacan) suggested that science tends to reduce all explanations to two kinds: meaning explanations and energy explanations (Wilden 1972).

Although the use of "energy" in the course draws on important theoretical traditions, in the end it represents a pragmatic choice of terminology. Since any name is a word, it is impossible to name "energies" without making them into themes. Nevertheless, the actual energies that the class finds at work in Richmond are commonplace and mundane; they are not unusual or surprising. Early in the course we watch the film *The Thirty Second Seduction*, which is about advertising on television. It shows some of the energies that businesses rely on to sell their products. Sex, fear, patriotism, and nostalgia are energies found in commercials. These and other common energies can be found at work in the crowd attending a high school basketball game on a snowy Friday evening in Richmond, Indiana. They are found every day in the agencies in which students volunteer. We look for helpful clues in the theoretical and experimental study of behavioral biology, the biochemistry of hormones, and the psychology of emotions — but our own study is more resolutely empirical. We find energy where we find it, in the lives of people in Richmond, and we try to gain insight into the energy we encounter. We then name it with a pragmatically chosen word or phrase. In looking at sources of energy, the students deeply examine their placements, making connections at both the theoretical and practical levels.

Advanced Debriefing

After about eight weeks, the team has made a set of card files containing notes on themes present in Richmond. A network of personal contacts in the community has been started, and follow-up work has been done to strengthen communication. Some of the information gathered has been transferred from handwritten notes to computer memory.

As the study continues, it becomes possible to move from making notes on themes to mapping the structure of a thematic universe. A structural concept that can frequently be applied or adapted is Claude Levi-Strauss's idea of "binary polarity" (1963). Students gain insight into how the people they became acquainted with divide their shared world into polarities. For example, students may find that on one side of a dichotomy are the "good people." These are people with families and jobs, who go to church and try to raise their children to do well in school, get jobs, and stay out of trouble. Threatening the "good people," at the other pole of the binary polarity, is the "bad world" of drugs, violence, international terrorists, unemployment, drunken drivers, pornography, perverts, unbelievers, welfare cheats, abortionists, and drifters. The students become able to examine these polarities through their service-learning assignments and their site visits.

It also becomes possible to look for "growth points." These correspond to what Freire calls "untested feasibilities" and to what Jorge Zuleta (Richards 1985) calls "usable themes." At growth points, a culture is already moving in a positive direction toward peace and justice. Four criteria are suggested for identifying a growth point: (1) it connects strongly with common sense so that it is felt and understood as meaningful; (2) it attracts energy from strong and vital basic sources; (3) it lends itself logically to transformation (such as transforming "family" to "the human family," or transforming by extension," e.g., "democracy" to "democracy in the workplace"); and (4) it leads toward positive structural change (Richards 1995).

Conclusion

There are other elements and topics in Methods of Peacemaking: readings, tests, computer exercises, guest speakers, discussions on fundraising and coalition building, nonprofit status, budgets, nonviolent games, political campaigns, surveys, content analysis, sharing of personal stories. This essay has concentrated on the process called "debriefing" because it is the most distinctive feature of the course, the feature most likely to help readers to see the links between students' service-learning placements and the aims of the course.

"Debriefing" in Methods of Peacemaking at Earlham College is a part of a rather specialized course linked tightly to a sequence of courses in a carefully planned program. However, it is the part that could be most easily borrowed for adaptation in other courses elsewhere. Although the guiding ideas of the debriefings come from the social philosophies of Freire and Gramsci, a similar process might well be used in courses with a different philosophical orientation. Debriefings could be helpful in incorporating reflections on service-learning experiences into many different courses in many different fields.

References

Berry, T. (1991). *Befriending the Earth: A Theology of Reconciliation Between Humans and the Earth*. Mystic, CT: Twenty Third Publications.

Freire, P. (1997). *The Pedagogy of the Oppressed*. New York, NY: Continuum.

Garcia-Huidobro, J.E. (1979). "Gramsci y la cultura." *Mensaje* 28: 828.

Gramsci, A. (1957). *The Modern Prince and Other Writings*. London: Lawrence and Wishart.

Groome, T. (1987). *Christian Religious Education: Sharing Our Story and Vision*. San Francisco, CA: Harper & Row.

Husserl, E. (1931). *Ideas*. New York, NY: Macmillan.

————. (1970). *The Crisis of the European Sciences*. Evanston, IL: Northwestern University Press.

Jacoby, B., and Associates, eds. (1996). *Service-Learning in Higher Education: Concepts and Practices*. San Francisco, CA: Jossey-Bass.

Levi-Strauss, C. (1963). *Structural Anthropology*. New York, NY: Basic Books.

Richards, H. (1995). *Letters From Quebec*. San Francisco, CA: International Scholars Press.

————. (1985). *The Evaluation of Cultural Action*. London: Macmillan.

Spradley, J.P. (1979). *The Ethnographic Interview*. New York, NY: Holt, Reinhart & Winston.

Wilden, A. (1972). *System and Structure*. London: Tavistock Publications.

Teaching Attitudes of Cultural Understanding Through Service-Learning

by Mary B. Kimsey

This essay presents one example of how multicultural understanding — and thus peace — can be promoted in an institution of higher learning. Through a course taught in the geography department at James Madison University (JMU), students learn about the importance of culture in world affairs and are encouraged to experience another culture to fulfill a semester-project requirement. The course, Introduction to Cultural Geography, fulfills the Global Studies portion of the general education (liberal studies) requirements for JMU students. Global Studies courses are intended to give students an informed understanding of cultures outside the United States and Europe. They are taught in a number of different departments across campus. The Cultural Geography course, in addition to fulfilling the global studies requirement, is a required course for all geography and international business majors and a recommended course for international affairs and social studies majors. Every semester, one or two sections of Cultural Geography are offered, with a total annual enrollment of at least 150 students.

Teaching Cultural Understanding Through Geography

In the Cultural Geography course, many different aspects of culture are discussed. Culture is learned behavior influenced by numerous aspects of human society: (1) values, such as ethics and morals; (2) attitudes, such as ethnocentrism and nationalism; (3) beliefs, such as religious ideology; (4) symbols, such as language, housing style, and clothing; (5) institutions, such as governmental and judicial establishments; and (6) social forms, such as customs and codes of conduct. Modern world issues including human population growth, global diversity in economic development, environmental degradation, and human conflict are discussed relative to the role that culture plays in each.

Although there is no formal peace studies program at JMU and the Cultural Geography course is not, per se, a peace studies course, there is heavy emphasis on the relationship between culture and conflict. Students are asked to explore the various aspects of culture that lead to stability and peace (called "centripetal forces") and the aspects of culture that lead to instability and conflict (called "centrifugal forces"). With almost every aspect of culture that is discussed in class — language, religion, political traditions, economic development, and environmental concerns — conflict is discussed. The "peace thread" that runs through the course is a discussion of the need for understanding and acceptance of other cultures to promote world peace.

To further emphasize this need for a genuine understanding of people of other culture groups, students are encouraged to "experience" another culture through a service-learning activity. The hope is that, through this exposure to another culture, students will realize that all humans share similar needs, difficulties, and hopes for the future. Through this contact they will, it is hoped, develop a greater appreciation and understanding for another culture group that will in turn lead to a greater acceptance of all human beings.

Service-Learning Options in a Cultural Geography Course

It is easy in the Harrisonburg, Virginia, community to find ways for students to be exposed to other cultures. The ethnic diversity of the Shenandoah Valley, in which Harrisonburg is located, is rapidly changing. Ten years ago, English was the primary language of valley residents. Today, one can hear a variety of languages being spoken, including German, Spanish, Russian, Khmer, and Vietnamese. All of these ethnic groups are blending together in an area of the state where the largest city, Harrisonburg, has a total population of only 32,000.

With the rapid change in ethnic diversity, tensions between the locally born population and the foreign-born population, as well as among the various foreign-born segments of the population, have developed. Violence in the schools, beatings, vandalism, and malicious graffiti associated with ethnic tensions have been documented.

The majority of foreign-born residents in the community have come from either Mexico or the former Soviet Union. Three agencies have been established to help with the settlement and survival of the newcomers. The Harrisonburg Area Hispanic Services Office and the Migrant Education Office work with the Hispanic population, many of whom originally entered the country as migrant workers. The Refugee Resettlement Office works with the former Soviets, most of whom have entered the country as refugees.

To complete a semester-project requirement, Cultural Geography students have participated in a variety of service-learning activities over the past few years through the aforementioned agencies. One semester, a group of students assisted the local Hispanic organization in planning and carrying out the first annual Harrisonburg Hispanic Culture Festival. They worked with the local Hispanic community to plan and set up exhibits for the festival. They witnessed the intolerance of some inhabitants of the area toward the Mexicans expressed in the form of a bomb threat and a painted message, "Mexicans Go Home," at the festival site the morning of the big event. For the JMU students, it was a major cultural experience.

More recently, a group of students assisted the local Migrant Education Office in carrying out a census of the Hispanic population. Students who spoke Spanish went door-to-door in the Hispanic neighborhoods to obtain information on family size, age of members, and employment. Students who participated in this project found it to be, as in the case of the project previously described, a great learning experience.

The primary service-learning activity has been, however, the tutoring of refugees in the local public school system. The tutoring of refugees in the schools began in fall semester 1993, with 19 students from the Cultural Geography class. By spring semester 1996, 40 to 60 students taking the course were tutoring every semester. Most students have been placed with refugee children in the Harrisonburg elementary, middle, and high schools through a staff person at the Refugee Resettlement Office. In the past year, students have also been assigned to tutor in the homes of refugees through the Refugee Resettlement Office or in the homes of former migrant workers through the area's Migrant Education Office. In addition, we are now receiving requests from teachers in schools outside of Harrisonburg who are overwhelmed with the growing number of non-English speakers.

Placement of 40 to 60 students in tutoring positions every semester involves significant organization. Prior to the beginning of the semester, staff members at the Refugee Resettlement Office and the Migrant Education Office make a list of days, times, and places where tutors are needed. Once the semester has begun and students have been given information about the tutoring program, they can sign up. Each student chooses a place (in a school or in a home) and a day and a time slot during which she or he is available to tutor. Tutoring positions are then made final by the local Refugee Resettlement Office, the Migrant Education Office staff, and myself. Students receive instructions from the agency staff on when to begin tutoring and what to expect in their particular tutoring positions.

In the schools, each JMU student assists an English-as-a-Second-Language (ESL) teacher with a group of students in his or her ESL classroom or works with a group during a study hall. In the homes of refugees, two JMU students work together to teach English to a group of adults, to a group of school-age children, or to an entire family. Usually the children need assistance with homework. If the children have no homework, the tutors will, through a game or activity, work on improving English skills. Many JMU students have demonstrated amazing creativity in working with their charges, some of whom speak little or no English.

Guidelines for student dress and behavior have been created and are formally agreed to by each JMU student. Very few problems have been reported in terms of dress, behavior, or attendance, though attendance has probably been the most frequently reported complaint. As a result, great emphasis is placed on dependability before students in the Cultural Geography class are given the opportunity to sign up for the program. Recently there have been concerns on my part as well as on the part of staff at the Refugee Resettlement Office with regard to the potential for sexual misconduct, especially in a one-on-one situation in the schools. For this reason, almost all students are assigned to an ESL class in the schools or are sent to homes in pairs. Effort is being made to be sure that all students are tutoring in a group environment to prevent any possible incidents of sexual misconduct.

Students are required to tutor at least once a week. In the schools a tutoring session may last 30 to 60 minutes, while in the home they last one-and-a-half to two hours. Each student has a tutoring "log" in which to record dates and times. Either a teacher in the school or a parent in the home must sign the tutoring log at each session. Sessions in the homes tend to last longer, because there is less structure and the session is seen somewhat as a social occasion by the immigrant families. Only students willing to commit to longer sessions choose to tutor in the homes. Although students tutoring in the homes often put in more time, they are rewarded by a greater immersion in the culture of a particular group than they would experience in a school environment. They see the family members interact, taste the native food, listen to the native music, and observe other native customs.

All students who tutor are required to keep a tutoring journal. In the journal they keep a written record of what transpired during each session and any feelings they may have had about their experience. The journal and the log are turned in at the end of the semester. Assignment of a semester-project grade is achieved by observing the number of times a student tutored, the effort that went into the tutoring journal, and the feedback that comes from the school system, family, or agency involved. Families communicate to the agencies, and the agencies communicate to me on how well the tutoring program is going. ESL teachers are in touch with me via faxes. A student who meets the requirements of one session a week and submits a thoughtful, well-written journal receives an A for the semester project. Many students do much more than is required of them, and some continue to tutor after the semester is over.

Student Reaction to the Service-Learning Experience

The reaction of JMU students to the tutoring program has been very positive.

Word of the tutoring program has spread on campus, and some students now sign up for the Cultural Geography course just to have the opportunity to participate in this type of experiential learning.

The success of the tutoring program is evident in the results of a recent questionnaire. At the end of the spring semester 1996, a questionnaire was distributed among students who had tutored. Sixty students completed the questionnaire. Responses to 4 of the 10 questions asked are reported in the table on the next page. From the table, one can see that a large majority (74 percent) of the participants found the tutoring experience worthwhile. Only 3 percent (two students) did not find it to be a worthwhile experience. Sixty-nine percent felt that they had gained some understanding of another culture group as a result of the tutoring experience. When asked if they would choose this project if they had the choice to make over again, 87 percent of the students responded "yes."

Written comments compiled from the tutoring questionnaire illustrate how excited many of the students have been about their tutoring experience. Some said that every student at the university would benefit from this program, and others said that they learned more than the children they were tutoring. Many stated that they were sad at the end of the semester when they had to say good-bye to their charges, and some exchanged cards or gifts.

During the course of the semester, students who have chosen the tutoring option are asked to report to the class. They describe their achievements and their failures. Other students give advice and consolation. They discuss the relationship of some aspect of the tutoring experience to topics discussed in class. For example, when discussing "ebonics" or the establishment of English as the official language in this country, the "tutors" in the class call upon their experience in the ESL classrooms. When we discuss issues related to migration and the U.S.-Mexico border, students think about these issues in relation to the Mexicans whom they are tutoring.

Although the vast majority of students have positive experiences tutoring, a few complaints are made each semester about the program. Some students working in the schools have felt that they are given inadequate instruction from the teacher in terms of material to cover and methodology to use. There is a requirement to tutor at least 10 times during the semester. As a result, some students have complained of the problems caused by early dismissals at the schools and cancellation of school because of snow and flooding. In a couple of the homes, students felt as if they were baby-sitting because no adults were present in a house full of children.

As we are made aware of these problems, we attempt to come up with solutions, usually with positive results. The greatest problem facing the use of service-learning in the Cultural Geography course, however, is the

End-of-the-Semester Tutoring Questionnaire Results

How would you rate the overall tutoring experience?

    No. of respondents: 60

    Responses: very worthwhile   (74%)

                somewhat worthwhile   (23%)

                not very worthwhile   (3%)

                not at all worthwhile   (0%)

Do you feel that your understanding of other culture groups has increased because of this experience?

    No. of respondents: 60

    Responses: yes   (69%)

                no   (13%)

                not sure   (18%)

How much do you think your student(s) benefited from the tutoring?

    No. of respondees: 60

    Responses: a lot   (57%)

                a little bit   (40%)

                not much   (3%)

                not at all   (0%)

If you had it to do over again, would you choose the tutoring option for your semester project?

    No. of respondees: 60

    Responses: yes   (87%)

                no   (6%)

                not sure   (7%)

demand for opportunities. It is difficult to find enough positions to accommodate the large number of students who request a service-learning placement. In addition, it is a real challenge every semester to rapidly make assignments and get all the service-learning projects under way before too many weeks have passed. However, the excitement of the students over their service-learning experiences makes it all worth it and indicates to me that I have to find as many opportunities as possible. In the future I would like to have service-learning opportunities outside of rural Virginia. If possible, I would like to arrange an experience in the downtown Richmond schools or a spring-break experience in a developing country.

Summary

Cultural differences and misunderstandings are major forces behind conflict. In an effort to promote peace in the world, there must be greater emphasis on cultural understanding. Education, especially experiential education, can be a primary vehicle for promoting peace through cultural understanding.

Service-learning through the Introduction to Cultural Geography class at James Madison University has been a tremendous success. JMU students have praised the experiential learning aspect of the course. They see the results of their efforts as their young charges, who initially speak no English, eventually learn to read. They learn about the struggles of these new immigrants and see the beauties of a foreign culture. Students who tutor in the homes try new foods, hear unfamiliar music, and learn bits of another language. Through the experience, they develop a better understanding of another culture group, an understanding that they will, it is hoped, carry with them into the world when they leave the university.

A Mini-Internship in an Introductory Peace Studies Course:
Contributions to Service-Learning

by John MacDougall

In this essay, I discuss a mini-internship assignment I use in my course, Peacemaking Alternatives: An Introduction to Peace Studies, at the University of Massachusetts-Lowell (UML). Before describing the mini-internship, I briefly describe the university, the course, and the connections between the mini-internship and our peace studies activities. At the end of the essay, I assess the mini-internship's contributions to service-learning.

Peace Studies at the University of Massachusetts-Lowell

Until 1975 the University of Massachusetts-Lowell was two separate institutions — Lowell Technological Institute and Lowell State College. It is now a midsized state university with particular strengths in engineering and other technical and professional fields. Undergraduates at UML are mostly commuters, and their parents typically did not attend college.

We have offered an undergraduate minor in peace and conflict studies since 1988. It requires that students take both Peacemaking Alternatives and a capstone seminar, together with four to six other courses from a list of offerings in various departments. Unfortunately, the minor attracts only one or two students a year, largely because both university policies and the campus culture provide little encouragement for interdisciplinary minors in the liberal arts.

However, another vibrant focus of peace studies exists on campus: the Peace and Conflict Studies Institute (PACSI). This was founded after the Gulf War (1991) with the objective of promoting all kinds of public education on both local and global peace issues. PACSI's codirectors, in addition to me, include a campus chaplain and two members of the Department of Environmental, Earth and Atmospheric Sciences. The institute organizes three panel discussions a semester, with speakers usually drawn from the university community; for instance, a faculty member who has been on many solidarity delegations to Haiti, together with a Haitian student. In addition, with the help of several small grants from inside the university, PACSI has helped organize various conferences and workshops on issues of local concern, principally defense conversion and conflict resolution. Between 1993 and

1997, about 12 students in the mini-internship program have helped organize these events.

Peacemaking Alternatives: A Brief Description

I have taught this course one semester a year since 1990. Usually I run two sections, with an average enrollment of about 25 per section. The course has a 200 number and meets university general education requirements in the social sciences and in value analysis. Partly because of the course's general education designation, it enrolls students from all over the university, though the largest group is composed of sociology and psychology majors.

The course is intended to be a survey that is as challenging and informative as possible. Its main goals are to expose students to peacemaking visions and concrete programs and to give them some practical exposure to peacemaking initiatives. It is frequently suggested to students that an enormous amount can be learned from "ordinary people" in addition to what can be learned from political and economic leaders. Accordingly, all these topics are examined at local, national, and global levels.

We spend about a month on a brief consideration of the context of peacemaking, especially on militarism as a case of the "bad news," and peace and allied movements as a case of the "good news." The remainder of the course consists of a "menu" of important peacemaking approaches and issue areas. These include local and international conflict resolution, environmental issues, social justice, nonviolence, disarmament, and the United Nations.

In addition to the paper on the mini-internship, described below, students' written assignments include six multiple-choice quizzes; a journal in four installments, containing comments on readings, classes, and events (personal or political) outside class; and a final project that consists of (a) two pages summarizing and reflecting on three major points in the course and (b) either a short research paper, a second mini-internship report, or an analysis of recent newspaper clippings in light of World Military and Social Expenditures (Sivard 1996).

The Mini-Internship Assignment

The goal of the mini-internship (MI) is to give students significant experiential exposure to the *practice* of peacemaking, broadly conceived, and to encourage students to reflect carefully on this exposure. To this end, students have two options for their midsemester projects.

The first is an interview with an activist. The procedures for locating interviewees, and for my approving them, are very similar to those for the MI. In the interview itself, the main topics students must include are the activist's primary accomplishments and values. In their three-page reports, students summarize the main points of the interview and evaluate the contributions of the interviewee and her or his agency to countering structural violence.

The second option for meeting the experiential requirement is the MI. (See "Mini-Internship Assignment" at the end of this essay.) Ideally I would require all students to take MIs, but given how busy many students are with both school and jobs, I have made it an option. I give different weights to the MI and to the interview in terms of their contributions to students' final grades, since the MI involves more work. The interview report counts for 20 percent of the final grade, while the MI report counts for 25 percent. To compensate for this difference, I require more work of those doing interviews when they do their final project, so that for these students the final project constitutes 25 percent of their grade, while for mini-interns it counts for 20 percent.

Mini-interns must serve 10 to 15 hours at an organization. This may be on or off campus, either in fields directly connected to peace, such as disarmament, or in related fields such as the environment or poverty. Peace activism involves empowering people rather than "helping" them (a major point in Peavey [1986], the main course text) and frequently challenges the status quo. Because I want students to have experiences of this kind of service, I urge them to work with change-oriented agencies. Organizations engaged in lobbying or public education, for example, provide service through advocacy. When the MI site is primarily a direct-service type of agency, I require more details from students before their MI project is approved. For instance, a student who chooses a homeless shelter can serve meals as part of his or her service, but must also, for example, attend meetings with residents to help them find permanent housing and jobs. Almost invariably MI sites cooperate in allowing students to provide this kind of service.

After completing their site work, mini-interns must write a 3- to 5-page paper in which they summarize the work done, describe the organization they worked for, and assess whether that organization had what could be called a peacemaking culture and structure. At the end of the semester, students can do a second MI as part of the final project. They write a paper shorter than, but otherwise similar to, that required for the first MI.

Implementing the Mini-Internship

Over the years, largely because of the community projects I have undertaken through PACSI, I have developed relationships with dozens of agencies in the Merrimack Valley region and also with university colleagues involved in community work. Hence, finding possible MI sites is not a problem. Every semester I send a letter to about 20 agencies requesting their cooperation. I have only rarely had agencies refuse to place mini-interns, though sometimes agencies relocate, shift their focus, or require prior training that makes MI placements impractical for my course.

Since in many cases I know individuals at the MI sites, and since the amount of student work required is quite small and not very sophisticated, I have no additional regular contact with the agencies once the MI has been set up. I do, however, usually receive comments — almost always positive — from people at several sites. When students choose their own sites at agencies with which I am unfamiliar, there is not much chance of students or agencies abusing the MI assignment, given its limited scope. In addition, the agencies students choose on their own are usually well known in the community. When a student seeks approval for a placement, rarely must I reject her or his request because the agency is simply not appropriate.

Although relations with MI sites require little effort on my part, those with students require much more. In order to maintain high standards, I give students a fair amount of guidance. This happens in several stages and in various forms.

In about the second week of the semester, I give out the instruction sheets for both the MI and the interview assignment. Approximately a week later, I spend a class period going over possible MI sites. I distribute to everyone my own brief list of possible sites, and I offer to interested students a comprehensive booklet on service opportunities put together by the UML's Office of Community Service.

A digression is in order here about teaching assistants (TAs). Since 1991, I have included as TAs good students from various majors who have already taken the course. They are unpaid but receive practicum or directed-studies credit. TAs do no grading but serve as invaluable bridges between the students and me. Since TAs have usually chosen MIs when they first took the course, they often succeed in persuading students to choose the MI option and provide useful information about possible sites. In addition, TAs often develop close relationships with several mini-interns and thus can help me maintain high standards.

Popular off-campus sites have included homeless shelters, the Lawrence Grassroots Initiative, and Rape Crisis Services of Greater Lowell. On campus, several mini-interns have worked on environmental and consumer issues with the Massachusetts Public Interest Research Group. Students are encouraged to explore MI sites other than the ones on my list and in the Office of Community Service brochure. However, they are required to get such sites approved by me before starting an MI there. Each semester rough-ly a quarter of the mini-interns choose sites this way. This proportion is as high as it is because UML is a commuter school with many students having connections with local agencies and, in addition, some already have service experience. I talk with students before approving MI sites they have pro-posed; not only does this provide me with information about the agency but it also enables me to clarify the mini-intern's advocacy role.

The deadline for approval of MI sites is about four weeks after the start of the semester. Around this deadline several students get anxious about finding appropriate sites. Not only do I have to give them information and encouragement, but I sometimes also have to urge them to be persistent in trying to contact agencies. After approval has been given and the student has started work, I require a 10-minute follow-up meeting with each mini-intern. If this meeting does not take place, the student's paper grade may suffer. This meeting is designed to check into the kind of work the mini-intern is actually doing and to assess feelings of satisfaction or dissatisfac-tion. Usually, these discussions reveal that the MIs are going smoothly. But sometimes I discover problems; for instance, a student is behind schedule or feels discouraged at not "making a difference." When such feelings arise, I remind students that organizing for social change takes time and involves failures as well as successes.

I have never known students to put in a grossly inadequate number of hours (although no doubt a minority have done 8 to 9 instead of the mini-mum 10 hours). This becomes clear in my follow-up meetings with mini-interns and is probably due to the assignment's relatively small time demands and to the format of the paper, which makes it virtually impossi-ble for a student to misrepresent the amount of work done. To the contrary, a fair number of students get so excited by their project that they put in well over the maximum of 15 hours, for no extra course credit. I grade MI papers primarily for clarity, coherence, and their relationship to course ideas, not for whether students succeed at their MI tasks.

I also encourage students to write about their MI experiences in their journals at any time in the semester. Quite often this reveals their initial nervousness about this assignment and serves as an additional way for me and the TAs to address emotional difficulties as well as to clear up misconceptions.

Both in the middle and at the end of the semester I invite students who have done an MI to briefly present their work to the class. Usually about three to six students do this; on hearing reports from their peers, many stu-dents are amazed at how much positive activism there is in the region.

Accomplishments and Contributions to Service-Learning

Since I started teaching the course in 1990, more than 400 students have taken it. About a third typically chose MIs, although this proportion rose to more than a half the last time the course was taught, thanks largely to especially vigorous promotion of the MI option by the TA. A quite small minority of students have done second MIs at the end of the semester.

Many students have said they found the MI the most valuable part of the course, and some reported it had had a significant impact on their career choices. For instance, a political science major who worked as a victim's witness in the district attorney's office wrote, "I still want to go to law school, but now I want to specialize in criminal law. Through this internship, I have seen what the victims of abuse go through."

How does the MI contribute to service-learning? First, it is generally successful at making clear to students the advocacy nature of many of the citizen initiatives for peace, social justice, and the environment. As indicated, it sometimes takes time for me or the TAs to explain the meaning of advocacy as service, but students generally grasp it by the end of the semester.

A second important aspect of the MI is that students reflect on the wider meaning of their service. Given that it is a 200-level course, and that many students in it are sophomores or juniors, promoting a sophisticated awareness of this broader context is difficult. For example, few students gain much understanding of how civil rights organizations have changed the terms of the debate on issues such as affirmative action.

Still, the majority of mini-interns do end up grasping certain basic concepts and also appreciating some important generalizations. For instance, after several lectures on the concept of structural violence, students working in places such as rape crisis centers realize that domestic violence is a form of such violence through its connection to traditional gender roles; it is an important instance of structural violence.

The MI is modest in scale but quite easy to organize and very adaptable to a wide variety of courses. For anyone thinking of starting an MI program, I have three suggestions. First, he or she should establish contact with the heads of at least a few agencies both on and off campus. Excellent places to start include the campus office of community service; campus and off-campus groups working on gender, race, and environmental issues; local conflict-resolution agencies; and student-life officials.

Second, I suggest that an interested instructor try out an MI program on a limited, pilot basis. There may well be small seed grants to facilitate course development or to establish community-campus contacts. Instructors would do well to recruit energetic, intelligent students they already know, either to take the course and take an MI, or to be TAs. In that way, there will be, from the start, a core of good students with a strong interest in the MI, and the instructor will be able to take advantage of peer influences in leading students to take MIs and to profit from them.

Third, as early as possible, mini-interns should share with their peers what they have learned from MIs and the advantages of them. This can be done in front of the whole class. In addition, an effective natural place for such sharing is any situation in which students break into smaller discussion or learning groups.

References

Peavey, Fran. (1986). *Heart Politics*. Gabriola Island, BC: New Society Publishers.

Sivard, Ruth Leger. (1996). *World Military and Social Expenditures 1996, 16th Ed.* Washington, DC: World Priorities.

MINI-INTERNSHIP ASSIGNMENT

The primary goal is for you to do a little volunteer work in a peacemaking organization (where "peacemaking" is defined broadly), to carefully reflect on that work, and to write it up -- details of the required report are given below. Another goal is to help you figure out how key teachers in this (and other?) courses can be not only faculty, but people who are poor or otherwise deprived; and people in agencies working with the deprived.

Specifically, you must volunteer 10-15 hours in an organization to be arranged with me. It's OK for groups of 2 or more students to work together; they can write a joint project report provided they check with me.

You can work in an organization opposed to war or pollution, or seeking disarmament/women's rights/interracial harmony/low-income housing; or some other kind of advocacy organization, PROVIDED the organization does not use or advocate violence. You can look for possible organizations to work in, or you can pick an organization from a list of ones I've contacted. It's very unlikely that a business or law-enforcement organization will be an acceptable place for your mini-internship. Your assignment might be setting up logistics for a meeting or other event; getting out a big mailing, etc. The work may be, to a considerable extent, just routine labor, but it should not be entirely routine. I have also asked your "supervisor" to let you participate as much as possible in the total life of the organization -- e.g. to invite you to join other staff for meals/parties, to attend staff meetings, etc.

Graded out of max. 125 points.

> **TO SET UP A MINI-INTERNSHIP,** you must see me by 2/18 -- preferably you should see me much earlier.

> **YOU MUST ALSO MEET WITH ME** at least once after you start the mini-internship, at a time TBA. If you don't meet me, your grade on your final report will suffer.

> **YOU MUST WRITE A REPORT,** 3-5 pages typed double-spaced -- 5-7 pages if you do a joint paper with another student who did a mini-internship at the same place as you. Your paper must cover the following -- **CLEARLY LABEL EACH PART AS** a, b, c, etc.:

> > a) the work you did -- the main project(s) you completed, a typical day at your workplace, etc.; also **CLEARLY IDENTIFY** the organization you worked at, and give the name of your supervisor -- take 1-2 pages for this section of your report.

> > b) briefly describe the organization you worked for -- its goals, activities, history, etc. -- in 1-2 pages.

> > c) about a page on the extent to which the organization you worked at is part of what might be called an alternative peacemaking culture/structure. For e. g., does the

MacDougall 1

organization deliberately avoid militaristic/competitive language and talk of peacemaking, non-violence, etc.? Is its internal structure democratic and participatory? Do staff and/or volunteers practice lifestyles that are nurturing, non-racist, non-sexist, ecological, personally supportive, etc.? Do they turn to other "alternative" organizations/individuals as their primary sources of political information/organizational advice, and for emotional or spiritual support?

*d) **OPTIONAL** -- discuss the relationship between the organization's _formal_ goals and its _actual_ activities, and CITE one or two of your own experiences with the organization.

*e) **OPTIONAL** -- has this experience changed your goals for school and/or your career? Has it changed your views on peacemaking? If it changed either or both of these, how?

f) **REQUIRED APPENDIX** -- literature of the organization -- as much as possible, please! This does not count towards the maximum length requirement.

*You can take up to 2 extra pages for parts (d) and (e) combined.

NOTES:

1. Two students can work together on their papers if they work in the same organization. In that case part (a) of their paper should be twice as long, i.e. 2-4 pages; and the whole paper should be 5-7 pages.

2. Spelling, grammar, punctuation -- be careful about this! If I find more than 10 mistakes in this area, I will take points off your final grade. Hints: (a) write **MORE THAN ONE DRAFT** of this paper; (b) show it to friends, roommates, tutors at **CLASS,** etc.; (c) use a dictionary.

Appendix

Peace Studies: Essential Resources

Selected Internet and World Wide Web Resources

The most comprehensive website for peace studies is
Peace and Conflict: The Home of Peace Studies on the World Wide Web
http://csf.colorado.edu/peace

> Begun by Robin Crews in 1992 as a gopher and ftp site in conjunction with his Peace Studies Discussion Group (see below), this website includes authors and articles; bibliographies; annual calendars of peace studies and conflict resolution conferences and events; calls for manuscripts; DFax News Digests; dissertations and theses; films and videos; funding and resources; honors and awards; jobs, internships, and vitae; journals; newsletters; papers; publications and publishers; and online syllabi.
>
> In addition, the website includes online guides and links to many college and university peace studies programs (including links to online course lists and syllabi), research centers, institutes, organizations, and networks. It also hosts the Peace Studies Association's homepage. This site houses the original peace studies virtual library: It offers anyone interested in peace studies a place to discover more about this interdisciplinary field. It also serves as a gateway for anyone wishing to discover the rapidly growing number of peace studies sites on the World Wide Web. Finally, there are useful "bookmarks" to help users quickly navigate the Web.

The website also houses the Web-based, searchable archives of the Internet-wide **Peace Studies Discussion Group** (peace@csf.colorado.edu) (also known as "**the Peace List**"). Begun in 1992, the Peace List currently has about 500 subscribers.The Peace List comprises peace studies faculty, students, program staff, representatives of national and international nongovernmental organizations, activists, and friends of peace studies around the world. Discussions on the Peace List vary widely: from issues of pedagogy, to suggested readings, publications, and films, to in-depth explorations of nonviolence, to analyses of current political/military events in the world (including, for example, the Middle East, Iraq, and Bosnia), to employment opportunities and conference announcements.

To subscribe to the discussion group, send the following message:
subscribe peace Yourfirstname Yourlastname
to the address:
listproc@csf.colorado.edu

Selected National and International Organizations

The Peace Studies Association
csf.colorado.edu/peace/psa/psa.html
email: psa@earlham.edu
The Peace Studies Association, Earlham College, Drawer 105,
Richmond, IN 47374-4095
voice: (765) 983-1386   fax: (765) 983-1229

International Peace Research Association (IPRA)
133.67.70.210/IPRA/IPRN_14.html
President: Kevin P. Clements
email: kclement@gmu.edu
Director, Institute for Conflict Analysis & Resolution,
George Mason University, Fairfax, VA 22030-4444
voice: (703) 993-1300   fax: (703) 993-1302

Secretary General: Bjoern Moeller
email: bmoeller@copri.dk
Copenhagen Peace and Conflict Research Institute (COPRI),
University of Copenhagen, Fredericiagade 18, DK-1310,
Copenhagen K, DENMARK
voice: + 45 3332 6432   fax: + 45 3334 6554

The Consortium on Peace Research, Education & Development (COPRED)
www.igc.org/copred
email: copred@gmu.edu
Institute for Conflict Analysis & Resolution, George Mason University,
Fairfax, VA 22030-4444
voice: (703) 993-2405   fax: (703) 993-3070

National Conference on Peace & Conflict Resolution (NCPCR)
web.gmu.edu/departments/NCPCR
email: lbaron@osf1.gmu.edu
George Mason University, 4400 University Drive, Fairfax, VA 22030-4444
voice: (703) 993-2440   fax: (703) 993-3070

Service-Learning: Essential Resources

Selected Internet and World Wide Web Resources

The most comprehensive website for service-learning in higher education is **Service-Learning: The Home of Service-Learning on the World Wide Web** http://csf.colorado.edu/sl

> Begun by Robin Crews in 1993 as a gopher and ftp site in conjunction with his Service-Learning Discussion Group (see below), this website includes articles; bibliographies; annual calendars of service-learning conferences and events; calls for manuscripts; definitions of service-learning; dissertations and theses; films and videos; funding and development; online handbooks and manuals; jobs, internships, and vitae; journals; newsletters; papers; publications and publishers; and at least 165 online syllabi in more than 35 disciplines (by discipline). In addition, the website includes online guides and links to many college and university service-learning programs (including links to online course lists and syllabi); campus-based service programs; organizations, networks, and resources; international service-learning organizations and venues; and K-12 organizations and resources. Anyone wishing to discover the growing number of service-learning and service-related sites on the World Wide Web can find links to them from this website. Finally, there are useful "bookmarks" to help users quickly navigate the Web.

> The website also houses the Web-based, searchable archives of the Internet-wide **Service-Learning Discussion Group** (service-learning@ csf.colorado.edu) (also known as "**the Service-Learning List**" and "**the SL List**") and archives of **the JSL List** (the co-moderated version of the SL List, which existed from January 1996 to January 1998). Begun in 1993, the SL List included some 1,150 subscribers in early 1998. The SL List is comprises a diverse mix of faculty, students, staff, representatives of national service-learning (and service) organizations, and friends of service-learning across the country. Conversations range widely and include, for example, defining service-learning; integrating it into the curriculum; issues of liability; benefits of service-learning, including retention, civic education, and leadership skills; sharing

syllabi in specific disciplines; program development and institutional-
ization; faculty incentives, rewards, and concerns; scholarship; service-learning semester break and summer opportunities; employment
opportunities; and conference announcements.

To subscribe to the discussion group, send the following message:
    listproc@csf.colorado.edu
to the address:
    subscribe service-learning Yourfirstname Yourlastname

Selected National Organizations

American Association for Higher Education (AAHE)
www.aahe.org
    email: tantonucci@aahe.org
    One Dupont Circle NW, Suite 360, Washington, DC 20036-1110
    voice: (202) 293-6440   fax: (202) 293-0073

**American Association of Community Colleges (AACC) Service Learning
Clearinghouse**
www.aacc.nche.edu/spcproj/service/service.htm
    email: grobinson@aacc.nche.edu
    One Dupont Circle NW, Suite 410, Washington, DC 20036
    voice: (202) 728-0200, ext. 254   fax: (202) 833-2467

Break Away: The Alternative Break Connection
www.vanderbilt.edu/breakaway
    email: brakaway@ctrvax.vanderbilt.edu
    Box 6026, Station B, Nashville, TN 37235
    voice: (615) 343-0385   fax: (615) 343-3255

Campus Compact: The Project for Public and Community Service
www.compact.org
    email: campus@compact.org
    Box 1975, Brown University, Providence, RI 02912
    voice: (401) 863-1119   fax: (401) 863-3779

Campus Outreach Opportunity League (COOL)

www.cool2serve.org

email: homeoffice@cool2serve.org

1511 K Street NW, Suite 307, Washington, DC 20005

voice: (202) 637-7004   fax: (202) 637-7021

Corporation for National Service (CNS)

www.nationalservice.org

1201 New York Avenue NW, Washington, DC 20525

voice: (202) 606-5000   fax: (202) 565-2781

International Partnership for Service-Learning (PSL)

www.studyabroad.com/psl/pslhome.html

email: pslny@aol.com

815 Second Avenue, Suite 315, New York, NY 10017

voice: (212) 986-0989   fax: (212) 986-5039

National Service-Learning Cooperative Clearinghouse (K-12)

www.nicsl.coled.umn.edu

email: serve@tc.umn.edu

University of Minnesota, Department of Work, Community, and Family
   Education, 1954 Buford Avenue, Room R-460, St. Paul, MN 55108

voice: (800) 808-7378   fax: (651) 625-6277

National Society for Experiential Education (NSEE)

www.nsee.org

email: info@nsee.org

3509 Haworth Drive, Suite 207, Raleigh, NC 27609

voice: (919) 787-3263   fax: (919) 787-3381

New England Resource Center for Higher Education (NERCHE)

www.nerche.org

email: [see form on webpage]

University of Massachusetts Boston, Graduate College of Education,
   Boston, MA 02125

voice: (617) 287-7740   fax: (617) 287-7747

Appendix

Contributors to This Volume

Anthony Bing is professor of English and director of Earlham College's Peace and Global Studies program. He also serves as executive director of the Peace Studies Association. His particular interests in peace studies include the theory and practice of nonviolence and the Arab-Israeli conflict.

Frank Blechman is clinical faculty at the Institute for Conflict Analysis and Resolution (ICAR) at George Mason University, where he serves as coordinator of ICAR's Master of Science in Conflict Analysis and Resolution program.

Robin J. Crews is visiting associate professor at Haverford College and an international faculty member of the European Peace University, Stadtschlaining, Austria, and the M.A. Program in Peace and Development Studies at Universitat Jaume I, Castellon, Spain. He is past director both of the Peace and Conflict Studies program and of service-learning at the University of Colorado at Boulder. He was founding executive director of the Peace Studies Association.

Robert Elias is chair of the Politics Department and the Peace and Justice Studies program at the University of San Francisco. He is author and coeditor of a number of works in peace studies, and serves as the editor and founder of *Peace Review*.

Andrew Garner is a Ph.D. candidate at University College London, and a visiting lecturer at Roehampton Institute London.

Michael Haasl is adjunct lecturer in justice and peace studies at the University of St. Thomas (MN). He designed and codirected a service-learning program at St. Scholastica High School in Chicago that also emphasized the "circle of praxis" format.

Michele James-Deramo is director of the Service-Learning Center at Virginia Polytechnic Institute & State University. Her scholarly interest is in resistance metaphors.

Mary B. Kimsey is associate professor in geographic information sciences at James Madison University.

Mark Lance is associate professor of philosophy and director of the Program on Justice and Peace at Georgetown University.

Seana Lowe is a doctoral candidate in sociology and assistant director of the INVST (International and National Voluntary Service Training) Program at the University of Colorado at Boulder.

John MacDougall is professor of regional economic and social development and codirector of the Peace and Conflict Studies Institute at the University of Massachusetts Lowell. He is starting a new research and action project on community sustainability.

Sam Marullo is associate professor of sociology and a member of the steering committee of the Program on Justice and Peace at Georgetown University. He also is director of the university's Volunteer and Public Service Center.

Martha C. Merrill is currently a Fulbright Scholar in Bishkek, Kyrgyz Republic, where she is involved with issues of university reform.

Howard Richards is professor of philosophy, peace and global studies, and education at Earlham College. Since 1972 he has been a consultant to the Center for Research and Development in Education (CIDE) in Santiago, Chile.

Anne R. Roschelle is an assistant professor of sociology at SUNY New Paltz, and the former director of the Women's Studies program at the University of San Francisco. Her book *No More Kin: Exploring Race, Class, and Gender in Family Networks* was a 1997 recipient of *Choice* magazine's "Outstanding Academic Book Award."

James R. Scarritt is professor of political science at the University of Colorado at Boulder, where he also was director of the INVST (International and National Voluntary Service Training) Program from its inception in 1990 until June 1997.

Michael Schratz works in innovation and change at the University of Innsbruck, Austria.

Henry Schwarz is associate professor of English and a member of the steering committee of the Program on Justice and Peace at Georgetown University.

Mary Schwendener-Holt is assistant professor of psychology at Earlham College.

Rev. David Whitten Smith is professor of theology and founding director of the Justice and Peace Studies program at the University of St. Thomas (MN).

Jennifer Turpin is associate dean for arts, humanities, and social sciences at the University of San Francisco. She is author and coeditor of several works in peace studies and is associate editor of *The Encyclopedia of Violence, Peace and Conflict* (Academic Press, 1999).

Rob Walker is at the University of East Anglia, in England, where he directs a program in higher education practice. Previously he was at Deakin University, in Australia, where he taught distance programs to students throughout Australia and Southeast Asia.

Christopher Walsh has recently retired as deputy principal of Whitelands College, Roehampton Institute London.

Kathleen Maas Weigert is associate director for academic affairs at the Center for Social Concerns, concurrent associate professor in American studies, and fellow in the Joan B. Kroc Institute for International Peace Studies at the University of Notre Dame. She has published and offered workshops on a variety of experiential learning, service-learning, and peace studies topics.

Edward Zlotkowski is professor of English at Bentley College. Founding director of the Bentley Service-Learning Project, he has published and spoken on a wide variety of service-learning topics. Currently he also is a senior associate on the AAHE Service-Learning Project at the American Association for Higher Education (AAHE).